A CASE FOR
BUSINESS ENG

Student's Book

Other ESP Titles Include:

BINHAM, P. et al
Hotel English* Communicating with the international traveller

BINHAM, P. et al
Restaurant English* Communicating with the international traveller

BLAKEY, T.
English for Maritime Studies*

BRIEGER, N. and J. Comfort
Business Issues Materials for developing reading and speaking skills

BRIEGER, N. and J. Comfort
Business Contacts

BRIEGER, N. and J. Comfort
Technical Contacts*

BRIMS, J.
English for Negotiating

DAVIES, D.
Medicine Developing reading skills

DAVIES, D.
Petroleum Technology

FITZPATRICK, A.
English for International Conferences*

KAY, V.
Biological Sciences Developing reading skills

LEBAUER, R. Susan
Reading Skills for the Future

McGOVERN, J.
Bank on your English* An elementary course in communication for bank employees

McKELLEN, J. and M. Spooner
New Business Matters*

NOTO, S.
Physics Developing reading skills

PALSTRA, R.
Telephone English*

PALSTRA, R.
Telex English*

PRODROMOU, L.
Medicine Developing reading skills

ROBERTSON, F.
Airspeak*

*Includes audio cassette(s)

A CASE FOR
BUSINESS ENGLISH

Student's Book

Michel Poté
Derek Wright
Armel Esnol
Gerald Lees
Roger Soulieux

ENGLISH LANGUAGE TEACHING

Prentice Hall

New York   London   Toronto   Sydney   Tokyo   Singapore

First published 1985 by Pergamon Press Ltd
This edition first published 1988 by
Prentice Hall International (UK) Ltd,
66 Wood Lane End, Hemel Hempstead,
Hertfordshire, HP2 4RG
A division of
Simon & Schuster International Group

© 1988 Prentice Hall International (UK) Ltd

All rights reserved. No part of this publication may be
reproduced, stored in a retrieval system, or transmitted,
in any form, or by any means, electronic, mechanical,
photocopying, recording or otherwise, without the
prior permission, in writing, from the publisher.
For permission within the United States of America
contact Prentice Hall Inc., Englewood Cliffs, NJ 07632.

Printed and bound in Great Britain at
the University Press, Cambridge

British Library Cataloguing in Publication Data

A case for business English — (Materials for
language practice (ESP)) Student's
1. English language — Textbooks for foreign speakers
2. English language — Business English
I. Poté, Michel II. Series
428.2'4'02465   PE1128

ISBN 0-13-115460-5

2 3 4 5 92 91 90

Contents

	Introduction	7
Unit 1	**Midnight Breeze**	9
Unit 2	**The Interview**	14
Unit 3	**Booking a Journey Abroad**	19
Unit 4	**The Delivery**	24
Unit 5	**The Right Man for the Job**	31
Unit 6	**A Recruitment Problem**	36
Unit 7	**Pricing Policy**	41
Unit 8	**The Production Line Case**	47
Unit 9	**The Crisis**	48
Unit 10	**Monroe Washing Machines**	52
Unit 11	**Wizard Electronics**	56
Unit 12	**Carter and Kennedy**	63
Unit 13	**Cross-Magill**	68
Unit 14	**Zilvanium**	74
Unit 15	**The Daltons**	94
	Business Briefs	107

Introduction

To the student

This course has been designed in the light of direct experience in what language skills are required when doing business in English anywhere in the world.

The basic assumption was that a business person will speak English to achieve a result and that in order to do so a rapport has to be established first with somebody somewhere.

Few learners nowadays still believe that there is such a thing as solitary language acquisition and that, in class, the teacher is the one and only fountain of wisdom they should tap. On the contrary, students should be well aware that they learn from each other in class and that this natural process should be encouraged.

If your teacher has selected this course for your group, this shows he/she is as convinced as we are that the only key to your success is your effort to get your points across to someone else: this demands listening and understanding skills together with a genuine interest in the person you are speaking with even when your interests seem to be somewhat conflicting.

Business people are often said to be the first envoys to enter a country. To do so they must have a keen respect for other people's feelings and interests. You have reached a level in your English studies where you will sometimes feel that at a given moment, the best way to speak English for Business is to remain silent and give your partner a chance to put his point in detail.

Now, if you subscribe to the above principles, turn round to your neighbour and you will see that the linguistic tools you have come to this class for—and that we have designed into our various exercises—will come to your help.

We do hope you will enjoy this course as much as we did while developing it with the invaluable assistance of several generations of our Business English students, to whom we are very grateful.

The authors.

UNIT 1
Midnight Breeze

This is the case of a shampoo, recently launched with an intensive advertising campaign, which appears to be causing some harm to its users.

1. What the papers say

Work in groups of three. Each member of the group should read one of the articles which follow and then sum up its contents for the other members of the group.

Evening Echo   29th January

MIDNIGHT BREEZE —a hair-raising story

While soap products millionaire, Henry Soame, takes refuge in sullen silence, 'Choose', the consumers' organisation, is filing hundreds of complaints from incensed users of Midnight Breeze shampoo. The shampoo was launched on to the market only three months ago in the blaze of an intensive advertising campaign.

Consumer complaints
Said Maureen Price of 'Choose': "Many of the complaints mention itching, heavy dandruff, loss of hair and unsightly inflammation. Most of the victims are women who have been misled by the slogan the company used: 'As soft as an evening wind, Midnight Breeze will caress your hair ...'"

Cynical advertising
Ralph Lado, the well-known consumer lawyer, called this "a typical case of ruthless capitalism on the part of a company which has made a doubtful name for itself through crude and cynical advertising campaigns." He continued, "If this company devoted only a tenth of what it spends on advertising to consumer protection, this catastrophe would not have happened."

Although the company claims that it has instructed its retailers to withdraw the shampoo from sale, it was still widely available in London stores yesterday.

Financial Daily   29th January

Midnight Breeze

Soame's Soap Products is well-known in London business circles as the epitome of a small company which has managed to carve out profitable niches for itself in a market dominated by a few industrial giants. Today that reputation is in danger as complaints about its latest shampoo, Midnight Breeze, continue to pour into the offices of the consumers' associations.

The company was founded in 1960 by Henry Soame, the present Managing Director, a brilliant research chemist who decided to go into business to exploit his own ideas. Soame's policy has been very effective: he has a knack for spotting gaps in the market and for marketing his products aggressively. With a hint of cynicism he is reported as saying, 'In the shampoo business the message is more important than the massage.' He has kept investment to a minimum despite the growth of the company and all production is still done by subcontractors.

Daily Times 29th January

Midnight Breeze raises storm!

Rumours about the possible harmful effects of the latest SSP shampoo, Midnight Breeze, were confirmed yesterday by the company itself. The Public Relations Officer for the company told our correspondent that there had been some cases of scalp infections but that a quick statistical survey had shown that only one per cent of all users were affected. Nevertheless the company has ordered its entire network of wholesalers and retailers to withdraw the product from sale.

Research chemists working on Midnight Breeze are carrying out new tests and the quality control staff is making a thorough investigation into the work of the production subcontractor. So far there seems to be nothing wrong with either the formula or with production process and the most plausible hypothesis which remains is that some allergy has suddenly come to light.

On the Stock Exchange today SSP shares dropped by ten per cent and there were further rumours of a possible takeover by the multinational conglomerate Prosper and Merrymay.

2. An early morning conversation

Listen to the conversation between Bill Soame and Irene Best. Note how each of them tries to avoid blame for the problem.

3. Pair work

Work in pairs with your neighbour. Choose two characters from the organisation chart below, one in a senior and the other in a junior position. The former tells the latter about the incident and implies that his or her colleague might be held responsible for what has happened with Midnight Breeze.

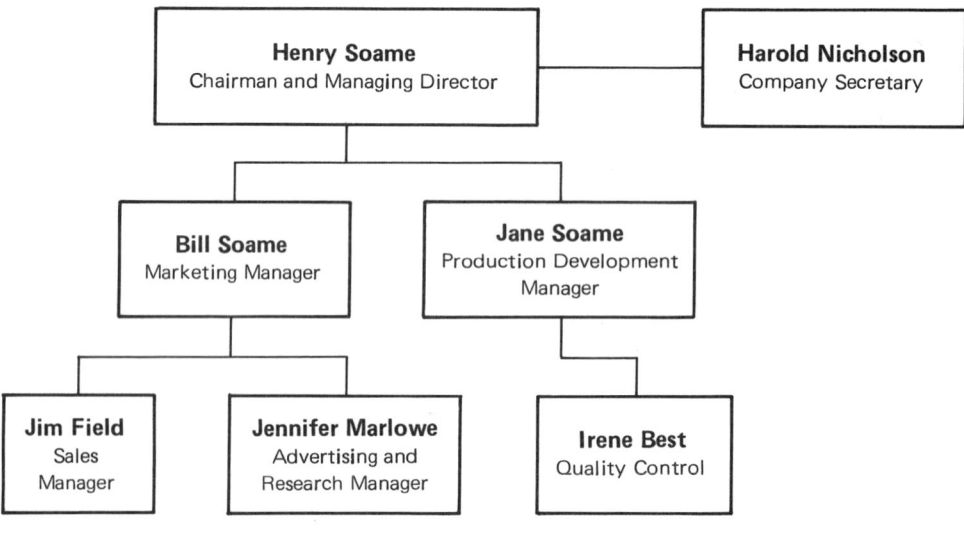

4. The defence strategy—group meeting

Having read the press reports, Henry Soame convenes a management meeting to define possible defence strategies for the company and to prepare a press conference scheduled for the following day. You have been asked to come along to the meeting with some ideas.
   What defence strategies would you suggest?
   How would you handle the press?
   Remember that it is still not known why the shampoo is causing infection or even if the shampoo is at fault.
   Write down your ideas as notes before discussing them with the rest of the class at the group meeting.

5. Faction meetings—managers and journalists

You are now going to work in two groups, one group taking the part of the company management and the other acting as journalists at the press conference.
   Management   Prepare one coherent defence strategy from among those you discussed at the group meeting.
   Journalists   Prepare the questions that you would like to ask. Choose a newspaper for yourself and imagine the questions that your readers would be interested in.

6. Private interviews

Although Soame has strictly forbidden members of the staff to talk to journalists, some executives were cornered by pressmen and forced to answer questions.
   Work in pairs, one as a Midnight Breeze executive, the other as a journalist.

Some useful phrases
The Midnight Breeze executive will be very cautious:
   Let's not exaggerate . . .
   I think you have been misinformed . . .
   Let's not get carried away . . .
. . . or he may hedge, that is, refuse to commit himself:
   I'm not prepared to comment at this stage.
   I'm afraid that information is confidential.
   Details will be released as soon as they are available.
The journalists, on the other hand, will be very persistent:
   Is it true to say that . . .
   Can you explain why . . .
   Can you comment on the rumour that . . .
   Rumour has it that . . . Can you confirm this?

7. The Press Conference

Still working in your two groups, Management and Journalists, proceed with the Press Conference. Henry Soame has convened the press and plans to give first an account of the situation and explain what action his company is going to take. Then he and his managers will answer the questions raised by the journalists.

Some useful phrases

To sum up a situation
Let me { sum up the facts . . .
          give you an account of the situation.
          make the following points . . .

To parry a question
  You have raised an important point there . . .
  I'm glad you have asked that question . . .

To insist
  You haven't really answered my question.
  To get back to the point . . .

To interrupt
  Excuse me for interrupting but . . .
  I'm sorry to butt in . . .

To express disbelief
  It's hard to believe that . . .
  Do you expect us to believe that . . .

8. For the record

Journalists   Write an article for your newspapers after the Press Conference.
Midnight Breeze executives   Write an internal memo or meeting report summarising the Press Conference.

9. Further readings

In the interests of health or safety, warnings like these may appear in the press after an incident like that of Midnight Breeze.

WARNING

PRINCESS MICROWAVE OVEN OWNERS

The manufacturer of the Princess microwave oven has notified its UK distributors Duotone International of a potential safety hazard that will occur in the event of a component part failure. The manufacturer advises all owners of the Princess to have their microwave ovens modified immediately. This modification can be accomplished very simply in your home and will be provided free of charge.

Please contact—01-906 8033/01-703 5248 for further information.

Important notice from Loma

WARNING

Loma regret to announce that, in a very few cases, faults have been found on their portable fan heaters. This also applies to Electro and Tonelle branded fan heaters.
To be safe, it is essential that these heaters are checked immediately. If you have one of these heaters, UNPLUG it from the mains. Look into the front grille with a torch or under a strong light. The faults you are looking for are lengths of element wire closer than $\frac{1}{4}''$ to any surrounding sheet metal (A in illustration) or long stray strands of copper wire (B in illustration). If you think you have a faulty heater or have any doubts, and it is a LOMA HEATER take one of three steps:
1. Fill in the coupon below and send it to Loma Electric Ltd. (No postage needed).
or
2. Take the heater back to the place from which you bought it so that it can be checked. In case of difficulty contact Loma.

ELECTRO OR TONELLE HEATERS:

If in doubt, owners of Electro heaters should contact their Electricity Board; owners of Tonelle heaters should return the heater to their nearest branch of the John Lewis Partnership for examination.
Immediately the faults were discovered, steps were taken to ensure that heaters now on sale are correct.

Model Nos. affected: LOMA 406, 407, 408, 416, 417, 418. ELECTRO 76RMA 406, 407, 408. TONELLE 75, 76, 77.
(These numbers are to be found on the back of the heater)

UNIT 2

The Interview

This case will put you in the situation of job finding and will lead you either to interviewing candidates for a job or being interviewed yourself.

In the preliminary stage you will discuss the important points when considering a job offer and study the relevant vocabulary through the model advertisements. Then the class will be split into two groups, interviewers and candidates. The interviewers will write advertisements, short list candidates and interview them. The candidates will choose the positions they wish to apply for, write their curriculum vitaes and letters of application for them, and then be interviewed.

1. Read the advertisements

Work in groups of four. Each member should choose a different one of the four advertisements below, analyse it and sum it up for the rest of the group. The summary should include a description of the job, the company, the requirements, the location, the salary and benefits, and the promotion prospects.

These four advertisements will only be used in this preliminary stage of the case but the language of the advertisements will be important in the later stages.

SALES/MARKETING REPRESENTATIVE

Australia

THE START YOU NEED IN THIS SUNSHINE LAND OF OPPORTUNITY

Do you feel you could make it to Sales Manager within 5 years? Here's your chance to prove it!

Australia is where the opportunities are nowadays and Australian Brewers can put them your way. They are looking for someone for whom a rep's job is just a stepping stone—someone with at least a bachelor's degree in a sales or marketing related field and aged between 23 and 30. We shall expect you to be articulate, possess skill in understanding and interpreting figures, and show a capacity for planning and human resource management. You will need energy, a good presence and "office hours" should mean nothing to you.

The pay is good by UK standards, and princely when you take into account Australia's low taxes and cost of living. There are also bonuses, an entertainment allowance and a company car scheme. You will get a subsidised pension and medical and life insurance. Relocation expenses need not worry you and until you have found the home you want, we'll accommodate you free. You would be based in Sydney.

Australian Brewers has the largest brewing operation in Australia and, with its many other interests, is one of the largest industrial companies in the country.

Start thinking about widening your horizons now.

Ring John Moore on 01-341-6294 or write to him, enclosing a C.V. at

**Professional Recruitment Services
422 Regent Street,
London W1**

and he will send you more details about the company, the country and the immigration procedures.

PRODUCT MANAGER

We don't expect you'll be with us very long

C £11,000 + car

Very long as a Product Manager, that is. Because here at Medway TV Rental, things have a habit of moving fast—like the rapid success achieved by our new feature movies on video tape and, indeed your predecessor's recent promotion. And we suspect that, given the right background your career advancement into senior product management could be equally swift.

By the right background, we're talking of you being of graduate calibre. Ambition, a logical mind and a pragmatic business approach are essential requirements, together with good communications skills and the ability to motivate colleagues and external suppliers.

This significant appointment carries a competitive salary around £11,000 plus company car, relocation expenses where appropriate, and a wide range of benefits.

If you believe you are a true professional who can make a significant contribution to our business and at the same time really enhance your own career, then please write with full details to:

Stuart Sutcliffe
Personnel and Training Manager
Medway TV Rental Ltd
P.O. Box 134 Bassett Road
Chatham

This appointment is open to men and women

Assistant Export Manager
High Potential New Appointment

Our clients won a Queen's Award for Export Achievement last year and sell their stereo equipment in over forty countries throughout the world. Half their sales are now overseas.

They are looking for an Assistant Export Manager to help develop and increase their sales of established and new products in France. This job calls for close and continuous contact with distributors, their staff and overseas advertising agencies.

Candidates, aged 23–28, should be numerate and creative, thrive on pressure, possess the communication skills required to influence and motivate a wide variety of overseas customers and their staffs. Extensive overseas travel—but for comparatively short periods of time—will be necessary, and fluency in French is desirable.

The salary for this position is highly competitive and the benefits and remuneration package include a two-litre company car, free life and medical insurances and a non-contributory pension scheme. Relocation support will apply if required.

Men or women should apply to Dave Collett quoting Ref 213/B

Professional Recruitment Services
422 Regent Street

DEPUTY PERSONNEL MANAGER

C £10,000 + car and benefits

- Our client has rapidly expanded over the past two years and looks set for the best year yet this year, with a move to new and larger premises, and exciting new products just out of the pipeline.

- They manufacture and supply the huge field of telecommunications with the most sophisticated modems and computer peripherals around.

- Due to internal promotion they now require a highly motivated and ambitious person to help them manage a quickly expanding work force.

- Applicants, of either sex, should be graduates or of graduate calibre, have a confident, persuasive personality, not be afraid of hard work and have the motivation required to join a young and growing team of dedicated professionals.

Ref DPM.23.
Please contact Peter James or Michael O'Brien quoting the relevant reference number.

Parnall Recruitment Services
407, High Holborn
London WC45 2OJ

2. Before the interviews

The class will now be divided into groups. Five of you will go through the process of applying for jobs and being interviewed. The rest of the class will be split into five groups of recruiting consultants who will write advertisements, shortlist candidates and interview them.

CANDIDATES

a) You are looking for a job. You will later apply for three positions among those the consultants are writing advertisements for. First, prepare your own curriculum vitae (without using your real name) and make three copies (one for each job you will apply for).

b) Choose three advertisements out of the four and write your three letters of application. Then apply for these three positions by sending one CV and one application letter to each of the companies concerned.

c) Start preparing the interviews. Imagine the questions you are likely to be asked and your answers. You will also have questions to ask.

d) When you know which position you are going to be interviewed for, finish preparing the interviews. To help you, read the following evaluation sheet which the interviewers will fill in during the interviews.

RECRUITING CONSULTANTS

a) You are required to write an advertisement. First, choose one of the positions described below (a different one for each group).

Firm A.—Assistant Marketing Manager
In one of the world leaders in the travel industry, to help plan and implement marketing strategies for a growing retail chain. Based in Bristol. £10,600 plus profit share, merit plan, annual salary review and, of course, holiday travel concessions.

B.—Junior Brand Manager
In a company marketing a successful and growing range of infant food and health care brands. The successful applicant will assist the Group Product Manager in the profitable development of one of the leading brands. Aged 22 to 26. Competitive salary plus excellent fringe benefits.

C.—Deputy Personnel Manager
For one of the leading manufacturers of vacuum pumps. The successful applicant will assist the Personnel Manager in the recruiting and the running of a quickly expanding workforce. £10,000 plus highly competitive benefits.

D.—Finance Executive
For the lending activities of a North American Merchant Bank. Based in London. £10,000 + benefits.

E.—Deputy Head of Advertising/Public Relations
Newly created position. The successful candidate will be involved in the promotion, protection and reputation of one of the country's largest companies in the food sector. Generous remuneration package.

F.—Senior Sales Executive
In one of the largest groups of independent hotels to help supervise travel trade and conference sales activities both in London and regional offices. £10,500 + car.

G.—Export Executive
In the country's largest exporter of Garden equipment. The successful applicant will further develop existing key accounts in France as well as exploit new market opportunities. £9,000 plus profit share and other benefits normally associated with a large group.

b) Then write an advertisement for the position you have chosen, using what you have learnt during the preliminary stage. Describe the company, the vacancy, the prospects, define the profile your candidate should have and give the relevant details regarding the remuneration package.
   Once you have finished writing your advertisement, post it on the board or on a wall for the candidates to read.

c) Draft a letter to send to the candidates you will shortlist (one per group).

d) Read the CV's and the letters of application you receive and decide on an order of preference.

e) With your teacher's help, make appointments to see the applicants you have decided on. Prepare the questions you are going to ask them and the answers to their questions. During the interviews you will fill in an evaluation sheet for each of your candidates. Make two copies of the following model.

```
Name
Date of Interview:
Time
_____

Married/single                    children
date of birth
Nationality
Health
Manner and Appearance
Education and Qualifications
Present Position
Experience
Administrative ability
Social ability, relationships
Initiative
Motivation
Leisure Activities and Interests
Present Salary
```

3. The interviews

Under the guidance of your teacher conduct the interview sessions.

4. Follow-up

Consultants   Now that you have seen the two candidates, decide which one you will offer the job to. Why have you decided on this candidate? What comments would you like to make about the performance of the two interviewees?

Candidates   Now that you have seen the two groups of interviewers, decide which position you would prefer. Why have you made this choice? What comments can you make about the performance of the interviewing teams?

UNIT 3

Booking a Journey Abroad

You are going to work in groups of three. Each person has a specific role to play and has details of his or her role. Do not look at the details given to your two colleagues: all information must be transferred *orally*.

The three roles are
i) a businessman preparing a trip to Europe over a 5-day period
ii) a travel agency employee responsible for booking aircraft seats
iii) a travel agency employee responsible for reserving hotel rooms, car rentals and train journeys.

You are making reservations for *next week* (very short notice) and this may complicate things. You are in Birmingham, England, about two hours by train and two-and-a-half hours by car from London, and you must complete the entire travel arrangements from Birmingham back to the same city.

There are no tricks in this game, and it is perfectly possible to arrange the necessary visits in several acceptable ways. However, remember that you must always arrive at the airport check-in at least 45 minutes before departure time, and that it usually takes about an hour to collect luggage after the flight, then another half-hour to get to the centre of a major city. So, if you have an appointment at 11 a.m., your flight arrival time ought to be not less than 90 minutes before (i.e. about 9.30 a.m.).

One last point: don't forget that Britain operates one hour *behind* other European countries. When it is 9 a.m. in London, it is 10 a.m. in Paris, Bonn, Rome etc. A one-hour flight from London to Paris therefore apparently takes two hours, whereas from Paris to London it doesn't take any time at all, apparently!

Once your roles have been allocated, spend a few minutes getting familiar with the information on your role sheet and make certain that you know what you are supposed to do. **Look only at your own role information.**

BUSINESSMAN

You are setting off on your trip to Europe in a few days' time, and you have all the last-minute arrangements to make. Below is your schedule for the week to come. Arrange flights and hotels as best you can to fit in with your requirements. Remember you are starting from Birmingham (about 2 hours by train, or 2h30 by car, from London). You prefer to fly with either British Airways (who offer you a discount) or Lufthansa. Check-in time, as always, is 45 minutes before the departure time.

March

21 MONDAY

Ducastel S.A. Paris (Courbevoie) 11.00

22 TUESDAY

Stiller Gmbh Geneva 09.30
Bollinger Gmbh Basle 16.00

23 WEDNESDAY

Münchener Grammaphon, Munich 11.00
Kassel Gmbh, Munich 16.00

24 THURSDAY

Danskelec, Copenhagen 08.30

25 FRIDAY

Management Meeting, Birmingham 09.00

Your usual hotels are
- London : Grosvenor Court
- Paris : Hôtel de l'Arc
- Geneva : Hôtel Saint Louis
- Basle : ———
- Munich : Hilton
- Copenhagen : Regensberg Hotel

TRAVEL AGENCY EMPLOYEE: *AIRLINE BOOKINGS*

You are a local travel agent who normally helps companies with business trips. You personally don't book hotel rooms (that's your colleague's job): you just look after aircraft reservations. Below are the details you may require. Please remember that Continental time is **one** hour **ahead** of English time.

	Air France	Brit. Airways	Pan Am	Lufthansa	Alitalia
LONDON dep. (Heathrow)	0800 to 1800 every hour on the hour, then 1930 2100 ↓ ↓	0830 to 1730 every hour on the half-hour 1915 2130 ↓ ↓	0900 1600 ↓ ↓	1100 1530 ↓ ↓	1420 ↓
PARIS arr. (Ch. de Gaulle)	2130 2300	2115 2330	1100 1800	1300 1730	1620

This is a 60-minute flight.
Pan Am/Lufthansa/Alitalia: no Sunday flights.

NB. At present, because of a go-slow, all British Airways flights at weekends are subject to delays of up to 4 hours.

	Air France	Brit. Airways	Swissair	TWA	Alitalia
PARIS dep. (Ch. de Gaulle)	every hour 0900 to 1700 No evening flights	1000 1200 1500 ↓ ↓ ↓	every hour 0815 to 1915 then 2000 2200 ↓ ↓	1130 ↓	1030 1200 1600 ↓ ↓ ↓
GENEVA arr.		1100 1300 1600	2100 2300	1230	1130 1300 1700

	Swissair
GENEVA dep.	0900 1110 1240 1500 1620 1800 ↓ ↓ ↓ ↓ ↓ ↓
BASLE arr.	0940 1150 1320 1540 1700 1840

NB. There is also a train service which takes about 3 hours: it operates 5 times a day, beginning at 0800 and leaving at three-hourly intervals (last train 2000). A Car Rental service also operates; your colleague has details.

	Swissair	Lufthansa
BASLE dep.	0930 1415 1710 ↓ ↓ ↓	0915 1210 1520 1730 2100 ↓ ↓ ↓ ↓ ↓
MUNICH arr.	1030 1515 1810	1015 1310 1620 1830 2200

	Lufthansa	SAS	TWA	Pan Am
MUNICH dep.	0840 1200 1630 ↓ ↓ ↓	Every 90 mins from 0800 to 1830	1130 ↓	0810 1215 ↓ ↓
COPENHAGEN arr.	1040 1400 1830		1330	1010 1415

All the Lufthansa flights are fully booked from March 19 to 28.

	Brit. Airways	SAS	KLM
COPENHAGEN dep.	Every 90 mins from 0830 to 1800 then 1900 2100 ↓ ↓	Every 90 mins from 0845 to 1815 then 1915 2030 ↓ ↓	All flights cancelled until further notice.
LONDON arr. (Gatwick)	1930 2130	1945 2100	

TRAVEL AGENCY EMPLOYEE: *HOTEL RESERVATIONS*
You work in a local travel agency which normally helps companies with business trips. You personally only handle hotel bookings; your colleague deals with plane reservations. Below are the details you will need to know, and car rental rates, for which you also offer information.

LONDON	**The Excelsior** (Park Lane):	£**40** single with shower
		£**56** double with shower
	all taxes plus breakfast are included in the price.	
	This hotel is fully booked on March 20 and 21 because of the Ideal Home Exhibition.	
	The Grosvenor Court:	£**24** single with bath/shower
		£**32** double with bath/shower
	breakfast costs £**2.50**p	
	VAT 15%, service 15%	
	No vacancies on March 24 and 25.	
PARIS	**Hôtel de l'Arc** (near Champs-Elysées)	
		19 390 FF single (shower or bath)
	Continental breakfast **18** FF	
	Service 15%	
	No Vacancies from 21 to 26 March	
	Le Royal Hôtel	**160** FF single with shower
	breakfast and tax included.	
GENEVA	**Hôtel Saint Louis**	**75** SF single with shower
	breakfast and all taxes included.	
BASLE	**Hôtel König**	**90** SF single (with shower)
	breakfast **10** SF	
	service 12%	
	No other hotels in this price range are available from 20 to 27 March (there is a large trade fair in the town). Other hotels are of inferior quality and are far from the city centre.	
MUNICH	**Hotel Europa**	**95** DM single
	breakfast included	
	15% service	
	rooms available from 22 to 29 March	
	Munich Hilton	**115** DM single with shower
	service and tax included	
	breakfast included.	
	situated near airport.	
	No vacancies 23 & 24 March	
COPENHAGEN	**Regensberg Hotel**	**200** Kr single ⎫ all rooms with
		240 Kr double ⎭ shower
	Tax & service included	
	breakfast included	
	Vacancies throughout March.	

CAR RENTAL RATES (Basle and Geneva)
All credit cards accepted.
Unlimited mileage available at weekends only.

Car type	Model	Cost per day (24 hours)	Cost per kilometre
1	Fiesta Renault 5	£15	0.07p
2	Renault 14 Fiat	£18	0.09p
3	Renault 20 Toyota	£22	0.12p
4	Ford Granada Peugeot	£28	0.16p
5	Mercedes Benz	£36	0.19p

All cars to be returned to the renting agency/town.
One-way trips have a surcharge of £40 (fixed rate all models).

Personal accident insurance (PAI) available at £3 per person per day.

All rentals include insurance, with a franchise of £250. The car rental company will assume this for a fee of £4 per day (Collision Damage Waiver: CDW).

Approximate distances
Basle–Geneva   : 250 km
Basle–Munich   : 400 km
Geneva–Munich : 600 km
Paris–Geneva   : 550 km
Paris–Basle   : 560 km

Trains in England
Trains between London and Birmingham operate every hour (including weekends) from 8 a.m. to 9 p.m. and take approximately two hours.

UNIT 4

The Delivery

Responsibility for lost production as a result of a failure to meet a delivery promise is the central theme of this case.

1. Transport

Fill in the gaps using the terms below:
   Some manufacturing companies have transport f_____, others do not. Most firms sometimes need to use a h_____, or independent c_____, to handle a c_____ for them when there is a need for an urgent delivery (or a r_____ j_____). The f_____ rates, or h_____ charges, depend on such factors as m_____, or whether a small vehicle or an a_____ l_____ is necessary. Clearly, it will be cheaper if the haulier can 'b_____' the vehicle with another customer's consignment to prevent it travelling empty in one direction. If the customer is not satisfied, he may c_____ the invoice. For example, he may c_____ against the haulier because the delivery time was not m_____, resulting in c_____ loss such as lost production time, or because goods were d_____ in t_____. In the latter case, the haulier is c_____ by his own insurance policy if the customer charges him for the costs of r_____.

backload	consignment	haulier	contest	rush job
met	mileage	articulated lorry	covered	
haulage	consequential	damaged in transit	claim	
fleets	carrier	freight	rectification	

2. Telephone call—a rush job

a) You will hear a telephone call received by Midland International Transport, a firm of hauliers based in Coventry. Read the following questions through before you listen, and then answer them after hearing the conversation to be sure that you have understood all the details.
   i) Which company does the caller, Mr. Daniels, represent?
   ii) Why does Mr. Daniels' firm require a rush job?
   iii) Why does his firm require delivery by a specific day?
   iv) What factors does Mr. Samson think will increase the cost of the delivery?
   v) Why does Mr. Daniels say that he will contact the French supplier?

b) Now it is your turn to replace Mr. Daniels, of Coventry Engineering. First listen to the conversation again, making brief notes of what he says, and then speak for Daniels in the gapped dialogue which follows.

3. Memo to the Production Manager

Write a brief memo from Mr. Daniels, Transport Manager of Coventry Engineering, to his Production Manager, Mr. Leadbetter (to whom Daniels is responsible), outlining:
   i) the problem with the French suppliers,
   ii) the arrangements you have made for alternative transport,
   iii) the effect on the Production Manager's installation plans.

4. Number work

Read the following sentences aloud, and complete them by rounding the figures up or down, eg.:   We have 296 vehicles in our fleet, say 300 . . .

1   We have 296 vehicles in our fleet
2   Our total mileage last year was 252,820 miles
3   We carried 2,961 consignments last year
4   We met 91.5% of our delivery times last year
5   Our freight rates have gone up by 10.1% this year
6   We did rush jobs for 205 customers
7   We only had claims against us from about 20 of those customers
8   We managed to backload 68% of our deliveries
9   Our total deliveries amounted to 31,041 tonnes
10   We could do the delivery for a cost of about £710

5. Using time expressions

Complete the following sentences with the appropriate word.

   We've been in business _____ 25 years; we've been specialising in international haulage _____ the 1960s.
   To collect those goods from France would take _____ three days, normally, but you should allow _____ four.
   You said that you wanted to fit the parts _____ Saturday? I'm sure we can get them to you _____ then.
   We always deliver _____ time. Yes, we'll have the parts at your factory _____ time for you to fit them.
   It will mean sending a driver off to France _____ a day or two, of course.
   The charges vary: it's more expensive _____ the weekend than _____ the week, and cheaper to travel _____ day than _____ night.
   Fine, I'll ring you back to confirm details _____ the end of the afternoon, or if not, then _____ the morning.

6. Telephone call: the delivery details

This is an exercise in taking down details from instructions which you are given, and then using these to complete a form.
   Listen now to Mr. Daniels as he telephones the hauliers with information concerning the delivery. Note down all the details that you can.
   Next, use these details to complete the International Consignment Note which must accompany the goods as they are brought to Britain. As Mr. Daniels says, you will have to leave some boxes empty for the time being.

1	Expéditeur (nom, adresse, pays) Sender (name, address, country)		**LETTRE DE VOITURE INTERNATIONALE** **INTERNATIONAL CONSIGNMENT NOTE** **CMR**		
			Ce transport est soumis, nonobstant toute clause contraire, à la Convention relative au contrat de transport international de marchandises par route (CMR).	This carriage is subject, notwithstanding any clause to the contrary, to the Convention on the contract for the International Carriage of goods by road (CMR).	
2	Destinataire (nom, adresse, pays) Consignee (name, address, country)		16	Transporteur (nom, adresse, pays) Carrier (name, address, country)	
3	Lieu prévu pour la livraison de la marchandise (lieu, pays) Place of delivery of the goods (place, country)		17	Transporteurs successif (nom, adresse, pays) Successive carriers (name, address, country)	
4	Lieu et date de la prise en charge de la marchandise (lieu, pays, date) Place and date of taking over the goods (place, country, date)		18	Réserves et observations du transporteur Carrier's reservations and observations	
5	Documents annexés Documents attached				
6 Marques et numéros Marks and numbers	7 Nombre des colis Number of packages	8 Mode d'emballage Method of packing	9 Nature de la marchandise Nature of the goods	10 No statistique Statistical number	11 Poids brut, kg Gross weight in kg	12 Cubage m³ Volume m³

Classe Class	Chiffre Number	Lettre Letter	(ADR*)

13	Instructions de l'expéditeur Sender's instructions	19	Conventions particulières Special agreements		
		20	À payer par To be paid by	Expéditeur Senders	Monnaie/Currency	Destinataire Consignee
			Prix de transport Carriage charges Réductions Deductions			
14	Prescriptions d'affranchissement Instruction as to payment for carriage Franco/Carriage paid Non franco/Carriage forward		Solde/Balance Suppléments Supplem. charges Frais accessoires Other charges TOTAL			
21	Etablie à Established in	15	Remboursement/Cash on delivery		
22		23	24 Marchandises reçues/Goods received Lieu le Place on 19		
Signature et timbre de l'expéditeur Signature and stamp of the sender		Signature et timbre du transporteur Signature and stamp of the carrier		Signature et timbre du destinataire Signature and stamp of the consignee	

7. Another call: the lorry is late

It is now Saturday 18th May. The time is 11.30 a.m. At Coventry Engineering, Mr. Daniels and his Production Manager are getting worried. There is no sign of a lorry . . .

Working in pairs, one of you takes the part of Mr. Daniels, who anxiously telephones Midland International Transport for an explanation. The other plays the part of Mr. Samson's assistant, who is in the office on Saturday mornings to prepare documents for the Monday deliveries.

Study your role card (pages 27–28) before beginning the conversation. **Look only at your own role information.**

TELEPHONE CALL: *ROLE INFORMATION*

Mr. Daniels
It is Sat. 18th May. By 11.30 a.m. the machine parts still have not arrived and you are worried. So too is the Production Manager, who is waiting to supervise the Chief Engineer and a team of fitters as they install the machine parts ready for Production on Monday of a new type of product design.

As you make the call to Mr. Samson at Midland International Transport, the Production Manager is standing right beside you! You must apply pressure to get the parts on time and to show your Manager you are doing all you can.

Among your questions may be the following:
    What has happened?
    Where are the parts now?
    Have the parts been lost or damaged in any way?
    Why were you not told sooner?
    When will the parts arrive?
    What about the loss of production and installation time?
    Why is Mr. Samson not dealing with the matter personally?
    What steps is the company taking?
    When will Mr. Samson be in touch with you?

During the call, you will be seeking information and trying to place the responsibility on the hauliers. Try to make use of some of the following expressions:

Pushing for information
I'd like a direct answer.
Don't try to avoid the issue.
I'm afraid that's not good enough.

Placing responsibility
What do you intend to do about . . . ?
I assume that you'll make arrangements to . . . ?
Presumably you . . . ?

TELEPHONE CALL: *ROLE INFORMATION*

Mr. Samson's Assistant

You are in the office on Saturday morning, as usual. Half an hour ago, one of your drivers telephoned from France to say that his lorry had been involved in a road accident (not his fault) on the way to the ferry port of Dieppe. The goods on the lorry appeared undamaged but some repairs to the vehicle would need to be finished before he could take the ferry. He was hoping to catch a ferry on Sunday morning, which would mean that he would finally get back to Coventry by Sunday evening, though he couldn't be sure.

Your first reaction was to telephone Mr. Samson, but on the phone his wife told you that he was playing golf and would not be back until about 1.30.

Now Mr. Daniels from Coventry Engineering is ringing you up, rather angrily it seems. Tell him what you can, but avoid committing your firm to any responsibility in the matter for now; that's for Mr. Samson to deal with!

Try to make use of some of the following expressions:

When you don't know
That's as far as my information goes.
I can only tell you what I've been told.
That's the situation as we see it at the moment.

Avoiding responsibility
I'm not in a position to say at the moment.
That depends on various factors.
These are things to be discussed later.

8. Preparation meetings

The class will now be divided into two groups of equal numbers, representing either Coventry Engineering or Midland International Transport. Each side will prepare its case with reference to the final role cards (pages 29 and 30).

Before facing representatives of the other group on a one-to-one basis, each group should consider:
a) what are their responsibilities for the various costs,
b) which settlement is the one which they will aim for,
c) which settlement is the worst which they would accept,
d) in which order to approach the various items in dispute.

9. Written task

As a basis for discussion, each member of the preparation groups should write a letter to the other firm giving his view of the two companies' obligations as he sees them. The letter must be polite, but firm: whatever you ask for now, you will probably have to make concessions during the negotiation!

10. The negotiation

Representatives of Coventry Engineering and Midland International meet to resolve the dispute between them, on a one-to-one basis.
   Participants should aim to:
a) Keep the discussion polite at all times.
b) Be prepared to negotiate for up to 45 minutes.
c) Resolve the issue rather than arrange further talks.
d) Report on all their decisions after the negotiation.

The meeting takes place in the offices of Coventry Engineering.

MIDLAND INTERNATIONAL TRANSPORT: *ROLE INFORMATION*
It is now two weeks since the incident in France. You have invoiced Coventry Engineering for the delivery of their machine parts but they have suggested you visit them to discuss the matter.

1 **Your invoice**
   At £710, this is higher than the £520 you last charged for a similar route, but you think it justified by the expensive weekend ferry crossings and the lack of time to obtain a consignment for backloading.

2 **Damage in transit:** Rectification costs £230
   Coventry now claim that the parts showed signs of damage. However, no mention of apparent damage was made on the CMR note by your driver or by Coventry on receipt of the goods at the factory.

3 **Consequential loss:** Fitters' time £120; Production loss approx. £13,000
   Coventry wish to claim against you for lost fitting and production time. While you regret the inconvenience, you do not feel it was your fault. Anyway, there had been no agreement to a penalty clause in the event of late delivery!

4 **Outstanding payments:** £2,790
   You have been advised by the Accounts Department that Coventry Engineering has not yet paid certain invoices, now 2 weeks overdue, totalling £2,790. You suspect that this could be a deliberate measure to add strength to their position.

5 **Be careful!**
   Coventry have been good customers in the past and you cannot afford to lose customers to your rivals during a difficult financial period. You can see that they are clearly, although you think unreasonably, annoyed by the incident. You must handle the situation with great tact, but firmly too; you may have to make some sort of gesture of goodwill.

At the end of your negotiation you will be asked to report the amount of money which is to change hands, and to say to which items it relates.

REMEMBER?
That's as far as my information goes.
I can only tell you what I've been told.
That's the situation as we see it at the moment.
That depends on various factors.
These are things to be discussed later.
I'm not in a position to say at the moment.

COVENTRY ENGINEERING LTD: *ROLE INFORMATION*

It is now two weeks since the incident with Midland International Transport. You have received their invoice but have little intention of paying it in view of the consequences which their late delivery brought about.

1. **Consequential loss: lost fitting time**
   You had three fitters, being paid overtime, ready to install the machine parts which did not arrive on Saturday as arranged. Cost £120.

2. **Consequential loss: lost production time**
   Because of delivery delay: 2 days ⎫
   Because of damage to parts: 1 day ⎬ Estimated cost: £13,000

3. **Damage in transit**
   This was discovered during unpacking of the parts, after delivery (and therefore not noted on the CMR note). Rectification costs: £230.

4. **The freight invoice**
   £710 seems abnormally high compared with an earlier freight charge of £520 for a similar collection.

A representative of Midland International Transport is coming to see you today at your request, and you must use this opportunity to resolve the affair to your satisfaction. You must decide on which points you will insist and how to put your case. Aim for the most favourable possible solution.

To add strength to your position, you have withheld payment on earlier invoices totalling £2,790, now overdue by two weeks. You have no intention of settling until this dispute is resolved.

At the end of your negotiation you will be asked to report on the amount of money which will change hands, and the items to which they relate.

REMEMBER?
I'd like a direct answer.
Don't try to avoid the issue.
I'm afraid that's not good enough.
What do you intend to do about . . . ?
I assume that you'll make arrangements to . . .
Presumably you . . . ?

11. Conclusion: the follow-up letter

If the negotiation is concluded, each negotiator should write a letter to the other party to confirm what was agreed.

If the negotiation was not concluded, each party should write an internal memo to his employer describing the stage at which the negotiation ended.

UNIT 5

The Right Man for the Job

In this case you are going to choose a new foreman for the machine shop of Allied Machinery Inc. Three candidates have presented themselves, all from within the Company. You have to evaluate both the job and the men applying for it.

1. The job

Foreman required
Machine Tool Shop
ALLIED MACHINERY INC.
Applications with C V to:
Personnel Dept.,
ALLIED MACHINERY INC.,
Meadowvale Industrial Estate,
Renton RN15 6LA.

STAFF ANNOUNCEMENT

Due to the retirement of Mr G. Goddard, a vacancy now exists for the job of foreman, grade 2 in the Machine Tool Shop. Further information is available from the Personnel Department. Extension 257

FROM: Personnel Department   **DATE:** April 18th

TO: All Members of staff

Due to the retirement of Mr GEORGE GODDARD, there will be a vacancy in Machine Shop n° 3 as from September 1st.

In compliance with Section 9 of the Staff Replacement Regulations, any member of staff who wishes to be considered for this position should submit an application to the Personnel Department no later than June 1st.

For further information contact Mrs Lee, extension 257.

J. B. Ellisdon
Personnel Manager

2. Telephone call—more about the job

Work in pairs.

Student A: You are a member of the staff of Allied Machinery Inc. and have read the notice advertising the vacancy for a foreman. You telephone extension 257 to get some more information.

You are 25, joined the company four years ago and are fully qualified as a machine operator.

You want to find out:
Who can apply for the job.
How applications should be made.
What the pay is like.
If there is an age limit.
If there is a time limit for the application.

Student B: You are Mrs Lee, a member of the Personnel Department, on extension 257. You have information on the job of foreman which is being advertised as vacant.

When people phone you should get their name, age and qualifications.
This is the information you have about the job:
Preference will be given to the firm's employees.
Anyone who has been working in the company for more than one year can apply.
The successful candidate is likely to be in his mid-thirties.
Applicants should collect a special application form from the Personnel Office.
The basic salary is £500 a month plus a special productivity bonus calculated on the average output of the shop that the foreman is responsible for.

3. The applicants

The Technical Manager and the Works' Manager are discussing the need for a new foreman in shop 3.

Listen carefully to their conversation and note down their assessment of the strong and the weak points of each candidate.

	Ralph Taylor	David Pullan	Eric Burman
+			
−			

4. The job specification

What is the job specification for a foreman?
What areas of responsibility does he have?
What are the qualities required of a foreman?

Work in groups of three or four. Discuss and analyse in *general* terms the job specification for a foreman. (Do not just concentrate on the three men you have just heard about.) Make notes of your discussion; you will need them later in this unit.

5. The manager's view

Listen to the conversation between the Personnel Manager and the Manager of Workshop No. 3.
Take notes on what you hear and then replay the conversation, working in pairs.

6. Choosing the right man

Read the Confidential Reports on Taylor, Burman and Pullan which follow.
In the light of what you have defined as the job of foreman, the qualities required to do the job, and taking into account all the information you have gained about the men who are applying, assess the three candidates. Who do you think should get the job and why?

ALLIED MACHINERY INC.

FROM: Workshop Manager n° 3 shop
TO: Personnel Department
DATE: 22 November 19...
REF: Annual report : Ralph TAYLOR

                    Confidential

Mr Taylor has been working in shop 3 for the past 5 years, after an initial period elsewhere in the company. He is the son-in-law of the present foreman, Mr Goddard, with whom he obviously has a special relationship. He knows his job well and is a good worker.

Although he does have a certain natural authority, he has one major fault : he is not always in full command of his temper. At his age (40), he could be expected to be a little more even-tempered. In addition, he makes no secret of his hope to follow in his father-in-law's footsteps.

He is well-liked by the other men in the shop, even though he can be a difficult man to work with. It is to be hoped that he will learn to control his temper, a factor which ought to be taken into account in the event of a possible promotion. In this case, it might be worth transferring him to another shop, at least for a short time.

N Curtis
Workshop Manager n° 3 shop

ALLIED MACHINERY INC.

FROM: N° 2 Workshop Manager
TO: Personnel Department
DATE: 25 November 19..
REF: Report on Mr E. Burman

                    Confidential

Mr Burman is one of the most outstanding workers I have seen in this company. Although he is only 28, in the 4 years he has been with us, he has shown himself to be a rapid and skillful worker whose standard of work is of the highest order.

He seems not to have been affected by the trouble he had with the union over productivity, but since he is a very quiet man, it is hard to say. He is very ambitious and, I believe, still regularly attends night-school. He spent his first year with us following a twice-weekly course at the local Technical College.

Perhaps because of his tendency to keep himself to himself, he is not a very popular person, except with a few men who know him well. Nonetheless, I believe that he has great potential which could perhaps be developed by giving him increased responsibility. He would have to learn not to drive his team as hard as he drives himself. However, I would recommend him should the company require a supervisor or foreman in the future. I am convinced he would quickly learn the new role, and would give complete satisfaction on all counts.

W. N. Chadwick
N° 2 Workshop Manager

ALLIED MACHINERY INC.

FROM: Quality Control Chief (shop 6)
TO: Personnel Manager
DATE: 29 November 19
REF: Report on David Pullan

                Private and Confidential

I have had the above-mentioned worker under my responsibility for the past four years. He has consistently proved himself a popular worker with colleagues, and has a great gift for getting the best out of them. He is a big jovial character who is always ready to help foreman and supervisors, and his humour has on occasions avoided what were potentially difficult situations. He seems to be a born leader, which may explain why he is shop-steward.

However, he suffers from one great weakness : he is not the world's best worker, and has often been guilty of poor production results. Whilst this is an important factor in the everyday running of the shop, I feel it would be wrong to overestimate its importance when other factors are taken into account.

Pullan's strong points (leadership and worker organisation) outweigh his shortcomings, in my opinion. If management is considering a promotion in the near future, I would strongly recommend that this man should be considered for the post of foreman, or perhaps shop supervisor.

Alex Mcalister
Quality Control Chief

7. Report

You now have to make a report to the Personnel Department recommending one of the candidates for the position of foreman. The report should be in the form of a memo addressed to the Personnel Manager. You should give your reasons for choosing the man you consider to be best-fitted for the job.

UNIT 6

A Recruitment Problem

1. Introduction

Perrymans (Metalworkers) PLC, is an engineering firm. One of its activities is the twisting of mild steel rods for use in the construction industry (mainly in reinforced concrete). The part of the factory set aside for this work is a small building at one end of the main cutting shed. Equipment has been set up which requires six men working in pairs to do the job.

2. An accident

a) First listen to the conversation between the workshop manager of Perrymans and the company safety officer. Look at the diagram of the twisting shed and try to decide what has happened and how the accident occurred.

b) Listen to the conversation again and then fill in the gaps in the conversation below.

Workshop manager	This is the second accident we _____ this month.
Safety officer	Yes, and it's the worst _____ the beginning of the year.
Workshop manager	I thought that _____ the fatal accident we _____ six months _____ people would be more careful.
Safety officer	Sure, but working conditions have changed _____ you introduced the new productivity scheme.
Workshop manager	But that has _____ for two months now and we _____ two major accidents.

c) *Pair-work.*
Now continue the conversation. Work with your neighbour, one of you taking the part of the workshop manager, the other taking the part of the safety officer.

The workshop manager feels slightly uneasy as he has often been criticised by his colleague for not paying enough attention to safety problems. He maintains that it's all the workers' fault as they don't follow regulations. On the advice of the safety officer he has put up signs in the shops and has even organised a training session on how to use safety devices (gloves, goggles, ear-muffs). But in spite of all this the workers are growing more and more careless. He thinks the best solution is to move the workers to other shops and hire new staff to start on a new footing.

The safety officer is worried as the safety record of shop 2 is the worst in the factory: accidents are up by 20% on last year. He believes all this is due to lack of attention on the part of the workshop manager who is too concerned with productivity at the expense of safety: the rates are so high that workers are bound to take risks. Moreover the workers are getting more and more dissatisfied and would like to be moved to other shops. Perhaps this is an opportunity for hiring new staff and giving them proper training and working conditions.

Note: the two men are at the same hierarchical level in the company.

3. A telephone call

A caller makes enquiries concerning the newspaper advertisement for jobs at Perrymans. Take notes of the workshop manager's answers.

Caller: Morning . . . is that the workshop manager?
Workshop manager: ....
Caller: I've rung to ask about the job you advertised. Could you give me any more details?
W.M.: ....
Caller: What would I have to do then?
W.M.: ....
Caller: Hot metal . . . that sounds like it might be a bit dangerous.
W.M.: ....
Caller: So there's no danger at all?
W.M.: ....
Caller: Well, thanks very much. Oh, just one thing: could you give me some idea of the pay?
W.M.: ....
Caller: What's the bonus for?
W.M.: ....

4. Selecting new operatives

a) *Class discussion*
Perrymans want to recruit six new operatives. Before considering the applicants, try to define the ideal profile for the kind of worker required. Discuss what you would be looking for in these workers and what essential qualities they require. What factors would disqualify an applicant?

b) *Groupwork*

You will now be working in groups of three or four. One group of 'experts' will be given special information about the candidates and the other groups will need to ask questions to elicit this information before making decisions as to which candidates to appoint.

STAGE 1

Selection groups   Read the applicants' CV's and extracts from their letters of reference on pages 38–40. Make a note of any points which you wish to have clarified by the experts.

   Experts   Study the further information given to you and be prepared to answer any questions on the applicants.

STAGE 2

Representatives of the selection groups may now put a maximum of ten specific questions to the experts in order to clear up any points about individual applicants which may worry them.

STAGE 3

In your group, try to select three compatible teams from among the applicants to work in the twisting shed. Remember that you must make three teams of two persons each and that it is essential that the workers get on well together as they will be working in the same shed and the job is potentially dangerous.

STAGE 4

One or two representatives from each selection group now meet in order to come to a unanimous decision on which workers to appoint. The experts should listen to the discussion and will afterwards be asked to comment on the decisions of the various groups.

5. Written work—memo to the Production Manager

Write a memo to the Production Manager informing him of your decisions about the new workers and suggesting pairings for the jobs in the shed.

	The Applicants *Summary of information supplied in CV.*	**Comments from previous employers**
	MENZIES Clifford Age: 37 • English born in Jamaica • worked in a petrol station, until 1980 when he was dismissed • slightly disabled	*I don't wish to ruin this man's life: I can only say I've forgiven him . . .*

LEVINE Harry
Age: 34
English
- Orthodox Jew and adamant about not working Saturdays and Jewish religious festivals
- a quiet man who keeps to himself
- a good team man
- mentioned that he has had trouble with his landlord

Harry Levine was with us for two years.
He seemed to get on well with his colleagues and appeared to be happy in his work.
It will be a lucky company that gets this man to work for it.

SAID Mohammed
Age: 42
South-East Asian
- recent immigrant (6 months)
- wife and six children
- has attempted suicide

Mr. Said deserves to be encouraged after all that he suffered in his native country. He is learning English quickly with the hope he can one day recover his former professional capacity.

JARVIS David
Age: not known
English
- worked for British Steel from 1965 until now

Mr. Jarvis worked for British Steel until the day when he was made redundant along with 200 other workers, upon the closing of the Hampton Plant. He has always proved to be a very capable worker and a powerful leader.

BARRON Frederick
Age: 27
Irish
- Protestant from Belfast (has only been in England for a few months)
- was foreman in previous firm
- interested in firearms

Frederick Barron was with us for six months and during this time worked conscientiously in the company. We feel that his resignation after an unfortunate incident was unnecessary and we were quite prepared for him to stay on.
Hoping that we can be of further assistance if necessary.

O'MALLEY Sean
Age: 42
Irish
- Roman Catholic from Londonderry
- is looking for a new job as his wife has just moved to take a new job in our town

Mr. O'Malley has always been highly appreciated by all the other members of staff: he has a very happy personality, too happy perhaps at times, but everybody has his own weaknesses.

ROBERTS Gareth
Age: 41
Welsh
- is said to have a very unpredictable personality
- references seem fair
- very keen on rugby
- popular with colleagues in last job
- has not previously worked in an engineering firm

Gareth Roberts worked with us for three years and during this time we had no cause for complaint. His departure over a financial matter did not surprise us, however. We wish him every success in the future.

COCHRANE James
Age: 23
Scottish
- racially bigoted (according to one reference)
- redundant at present
- good worker
- enthusiastic attitude

*We had no cause for complaint during the time that James Cochrane worked with us.
We can recommend him to you with confidence, particularly now that his health problem seems to have cleared up.*

UNIT 7

Pricing Policy

This unit looks at some of the problems involved in the pricing of goods in relation to costs and profits.

1. Costs, prices and profits

Fill the gaps in the following passage using the expressions below.

Most products are sold in order to make a _____. This is the difference between what the customer will pay on the one hand (in other words the _____) and the _____ _____ on the other. The supplier has to pay for _____, _____, and _____, to which he must add a _____ in order to arrive at the selling price.

One of the greatest problems for a manufacturer is to know which products should be made to pay for which fixed costs (such as lighting, rent, and so on); in other words, his problem is how to _____ _____ _____ to the various products. His decision can affect the selling price of his products considerably.

Another difficulty is that of rising costs. Should he try to _____ these himself, perhaps _____ his profit margin, or should he pass them on to his customer in an _____ selling price? Or should he compromise, and ask his customer to meet him halfway?

Whatever happens, he should try to bear his capacity in mind. If his prices are too high and the customer will not buy, his resources will be _____; if, however, his low price attracts more orders than he can _____, he will be guilty of _____ beyond his capacity.

meet	underutilised	overselling	overheads
allocate the overheads	margin	increased	materials
selling price	profit	reducing	
unit cost	absorb	labour	

2. A call from the suppliers

a) You will hear a telephone conversation between a salesman and one of his customers. First, read through the following questions based on the dialogue. Afterwards, answer the questions to check your understanding of the situation.
   i) Why does the salesman, George, wish to arrange another meeting?
   ii) George's company (called ....?) is facing increasing costs. Which costs are increasing, and by what percentage?
   iii) According to the buyer, Harry, some of his suppliers do not pass on all their price increases. What do they do instead?
   iv) What does Harry wish to discuss when George visits him next week?
   v) What do both men agree to do before they meet, and what is the reason in each case?

b) You will hear the dialogue again. After you have listened, try to fill in the words missing from the following transcript:

G: Well, that's that settled. There should be no problem _____ those orders. Oh by the way, Harry, I'm afraid we'll have to arrange a time soon when I can come and discuss our prices for the _____ year.
H: What, already? Come on George, you people at Renova _____ _____ _____ _____ only a short while ago!
G: I'm afraid so, but you know how it is at the moment. Our own costs keep rising. Material costs have gone up again—by 25% this time—and we have to _____ _____ _____ _____ to our customers.
H: Not all of them. *Most* suppliers manage to _____ some of the costs themselves.
G: But we're _____ increases in labour costs and overheads too, you know. Labour costs could go up by 20% this year, and overheads by at least 15%. All manufacturing costs are rising, and our prices have to _____ _____ _____ them; otherwise we'd be _____ _____ _____ in no time. We've already reduced our margin _____ _____ _____.
H: Well, you know our position. The man in the street sees his wages only going up by about 5%, he can't _____ _____ _____ high price increases from us. And then our turnover would fall.
G: Perhaps we could meet, though, and talk about this further?
H: Yes, I'd like to _____ _____ _____ _____ your price structures and see how you justify any increases.
G: Would sometime towards the end of next week suit you? I'm in your _____ _____ _____ _____ then.
H: I'll have to check in my diary. I expect we can meet around then, probably Thursday or Friday. I'll _____ _____ _____ _____ to confirm.
G: Very kind of you. I'll _____ _____ _____ _____ about our pricing policy before the meeting so you'll see what the situation is. All the best then, Harry. Cheerio for now.

3. Pairwork

Now re-enact the dialogue between George and Harry. The following notes will help you at first, but then try to manage without them.

a) *George's notes on points to raise*

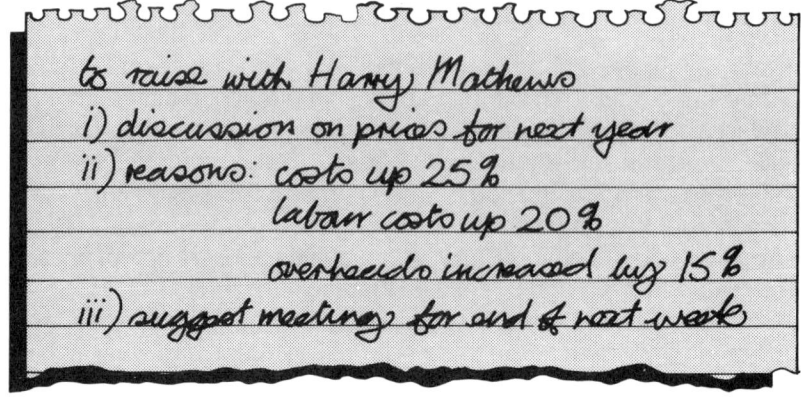

to raise with Harry Mathews
i) discussion on prices for next year
ii) reasons: costs up 25%
    labour costs up 20%
    overheads increased by 15%
iii) suggest meeting for end of next week

b) *Harry's notes on the points raised*

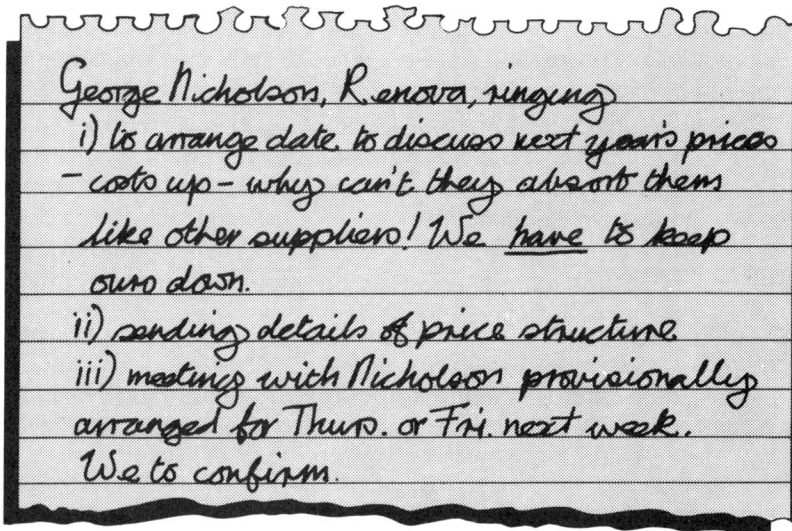

4. Letter-writing

Not long after the telephone conversation, both George and Harry sit down to write a letter to the other. The letter has two functions:
i) to suggest a time and date for the meeting,
ii) to set the tone for the meeting (ie. *seeking understanding* for their own point of view concerning the price increases, and *discouraging* the other from expecting much success for their point of view).

Use the following information and expressions to help you write the letter.

Harry is: Harry Matthews,
Buying Dept.,
Grossvendor Ltd.,
Norfolk Road,
LONDON EC1A 2BB

George is: George Nicholson,
Renova Ltd.,
Bristol Rd. South,
OXFORD OX3 0BW

Formulae
Further to . . . (eg. our conversation)
In anticipation of . . . (eg. our meeting)
I look forward to . . . (eg. discussing this with you)

Seeking understanding
I trust you'll understand that . . .
You will appreciate that . . .
You will know from our previous relationships that . . .

Discouraging
I don't hold out much hope of . . .
I think there's little chance that . . .
Without wishing to seem pessimistic, I don't think that . . .

5. Pricing exercise

a) *The background*

It is the start of the year and companies are busy deciding their new selling prices.

George, whom you have already met, is a sales manager for the small firm of Renova which manufactures a limited range of kitchen utensils. Renova make two products which we shall call A and B in this case study.

You heard George talking to Harry, a buyer with Grossvendor, one of the two leading stores which buy from Renova.

Renova is a public limited company and as such must make its statutory accounts available for inspection. Some figures, however, are more confidential, particularly those which affect a company's pricing policy.

b) *The company's accounts—internal only*

Look at the following data carefully. Say which figures you would expect to appear in the company's published accounts and which you would not expect to find. Give your reasons.

INTERNAL ONLY	Two years ago	Last year	The coming year
Sales turnover	£560,000	£500,000	?
Material costs	£200,000	£250,000	+25%
Direct labour	£85,000	£100,000	+20%
Overheads	£81,000	£100,000	+15%
Profit	£194,000	£50,000	?
Production employees	90	100	100
Production hours available	220,000	200,000	200,000
PRODUCT A			
Units sold	50,000	50,000	?
Material cost per unit	£2.40	£3.00	+25%
Labour cost per unit	3 Hrs. at £0.425	3 Hrs. at £0.50	+20%
PRODUCT B			
Units sold	50,000	50,000	?
Materials cost per unit	£1.60	£2.0	+25%
Labour cost per unit	1 Hr. at £0.425	1 Hr. at £0.50	+20%

c) *Trends in costs, prices and profits*

In pairs, take turns to describe the movement in these figures, past and (where possible) future.

For example:

Direct labour costs rose/increased/went up from £85,000 to £100,000 last year, and this year will increase (rise, etc.) by 20% to (quick calculation!) £120,000.

d) *Renova's price structure*

Using the above information, try to complete the following price structures for Renova's two products A and B. You are given their average selling prices for last year.

Then answer the questions below.

LAST YEAR'S PRICE STRUCTURES

PRODUCT A	PRODUCT B
Per unit:	Per unit:
Materials	Materials
Labour	Labour
Overheads	Overheads
Profit	Profit
Average Selling price £6.66	Average Selling price £3.33

Questions:
i) On what basis did you decide to allocate overheads?
ii) What kind of further information about the company's costs might possibly have made you change your mind about the basis of calculation?
iii) What kind of further information about the market for your products might have made you reconsider the allocation of overheads?

6. The negotiation

a) *The class will now divide into groups of 4.*
   Each group of 4 is self-contained and separate from the rest of the class. It contains:

- A salesman from Quickwork, a competitor of Renova, also supplying type A and B products

- A salesman from Renova, supplier of kitchen utensils type A and B

- A buyer from Grossvendor, a major retailer who buys from Renova and Quickwork.

- A buyer from Buckfast Stores, a major retailer who buys from Renova and Quickwork

b) Each of the four members of the group has a role-card giving confidential information with which to prepare for his negotiations. After the preparation period, the salesmen will visit the two buyers in turn, each meeting taking a minimum of 30 min. and a maximum of 45 min., as follows:

First meetings:

    RENOVA ⟶ GROSSVENDOR

QUICKWORK ⟶ BUCKFAST STORES

Second meetings:

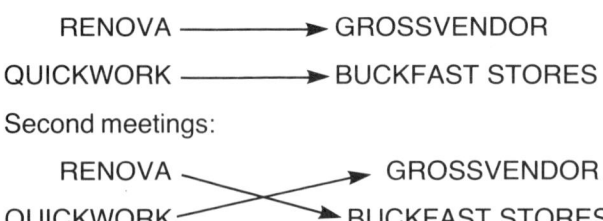

Between the meetings there will be a few moments for everyone to make any necessary notes or calculations.

c) After the two meetings have finished, the salesmen should sit down and write a short report for their Sales Manager on the terms they offered to the two customers and the orders which they hope to obtain. During this time, the buyers will decide, in view of the offers made to them, what quantities of which products they wish to purchase from which customers. They will then write a brief letter to each supplier, placing the order.

    The four members (or teams) of the group may then, now that the negotiation is over, sit down together:
      to exchange these reports and orders,
      to calculate their performance and compare with their competitor,
      to explain their individual strategy to the other members of the group.

d) Now, let's begin the preparation for the negotiations. It will be helpful to consider the pricing tactics with someone else, so, before working in their own groups, all the Renova salesmen should get together, all the Grossvendors, and so on, and read through the appropriate role-card together. You may need up to 30 min. to prepare in sufficient detail.

UNIT 8

The Production Line Case

For this case you are going to work in teams of six to eight and you are going to produce a piece of equipment which will be explained to you shortly.

Your teacher will give you a role card which defines your job and tells you what you must do. Follow exactly the instructions on your role card and do not look at the role cards of your colleagues.

The session will last about half an hour and you will be asked at the end of this time to give an evaluation of what you have done.

You must follow the instructions carefully and discuss any problems which arise in English.

UNIT 9

The Crisis

1. The office

This case involves two men, Robert West and Ted Taylor, who work for a shipping company, Hull Liners. It is time for that frequently sensitive office procedure, the annual appraisal of performance on which such things as salary increases and promotions are based.

2. Background information

Hull Liners is a shipping company; its Commercial Department is the responsibility of Robert West: he has six clerks under him engaged in arranging special forwarding of goods, such as door-to-door delivery, especially of containers. The clerks are mostly involved in routine paperwork: invoices, bills of lading and so on. As departmental head, West is also responsible for completing the annual appraisal sheet: this usually takes place in June of each year.

The six clerks under West's responsibility all perform identical jobs. When the time for appraisal comes each year, West therefore finds himself in a difficult position. As department head, he has to reach a decision, and not everyone deserves good marks.

TO: all Heads of Departments
FROM: Personnel Manager
DATE: June 22nd

Appraisal forms must be filled in and returned to the personnel department for June 30th.

You are reminded that the standard company procedure must be followed to avoid discrepancies between departments.

a) The Head of Department summons the employee for a short private interview during which the latter's performance is discussed.

b) The Head of Department must conduct the discussion and base his appraisal on facts.

c) The employee must be given a fair hearing but the Head of Department must keep his position of authority and refuse to start any argument.

d) The Head of Department fills in the form according to his best judgement.

e) Under no circumstances must the employees be shown the appraisal forms before management has approved them.

AW
A Williams
Personnel Manager

---

3. The annual appraisal—West's brainwave

Listen to the recording and then complete the following.

West had noticed that the three difficult men in the office were unable to accept d_____ or criticism and that they were always r_____ when he appraised them. They didn't seem to like his i_____. Their desks were always l_____ with papers, coffee-cups and cigarette ends. West was unhappy since he once got a r_____ from the Company Secretary because of their indiscipline. Taylor, the ringleader, c_____ they had no work to do!

The other three men, Brown, Harper and Morrow by contrast were very m_____ and accurate. They seemed to West far more m_____ and never complained.

Finally, West had a brainwave and decided to give the a_____ f_____ to the men and let all six of them f_____ them in themselves. That way he hoped to i_____ out any possible problems: it would be a d_____ between himself and each employee.

4. Self appraisal

Look at the appraisal sheet which follows. What does it tell you about the employee in question? Can you say what sort of person he is?

Hull Liners

ANNUAL ASSESSMENT SHEET

Department: Commercial
Head of Department: R. West
Date: 26th June

Name of Assessor (if not Head of Department):

NAME OF EMPLOYEE: Edward Taylor
Present post held: Invoice Clerk
Years spent in the company: 3½

	Excellent	Good	Acceptable	Poor
Quantity of work performed	X			
Quality of work performed		X		
Presentation of work			X	
Organisational ability	X			
Ability to take decisions	X			
Co-operativeness			X	
Punctuality	X			
Attendance	X			
Reliability	X			
Relations with superiors		X		
Relations with colleagues			X	
General attitude	X			

Would you say that this employee's work merits a pay rise? (Yes) No
(State reasons) Ted Taylor sells more container space than anyone else in the company. His work is of the highest quality

Would you recommend this employee for promotion? (Yes) No
(State reason) There are no weak points in the performance of Ted Taylor this year. His talents should be rewarded with a better position within the organisation

Further comments: Outstanding worker.

5. Office problems

Listen to the conversation in which West is talking to a friend about the problems he is experiencing at the office. Then answer these questions.
a) Why can't West go to see the Personnel Manager for a solution to his problems?
b) If Taylor really wants to challenge West, why is Taylor in a tight corner?
c) What is Taylor's most plausible motive according to Harry?
d) What should West do in this case?
e) What other motive does West advance?
f) What does he threaten to do if this is the case?
g) What is Harry's final piece of advice?

6. Case study

What do you think Taylor is up to?
What are the possible explanations of his behaviour?
What would you advise West to do?

7. Confrontation

First listen to the recording of the meeting between West and Taylor. What is Taylor's attitude here? Is he just joking, or challenging West, or is he dead-serious?
In pairs, replay this meeting. Listen to the recording again if you need to.

8. Compromise

The class will now be divided into two groups, the 'Wests' and the 'Taylors'. The former will interview the latter. Each pair should try to achieve a compromise acceptable to both parties.

UNIT 10

Monroe Washing Machines

🔊 1. Assembly shop 3

Listen to the conversation between Mike Lawes, a supervisor, and Andrew Kershaw, the Production Manager of Monroe Washing Machines. What is the problem in Assembly shop 3?

Now listen again and this time take the part of Andrew Kershaw.

2. The history of Monroe Washing Machines

Monroe Washing Machines (MWM) is part of a multinational company. The English subsidiary (MWM UK) operates two assembly plants in England. The largest one is situated in Southampton. The various parts come mostly from other MWM plants in developing countries where they are produced at low costs (motors in Taiwan, electronic modules in Hong Kong, bodies in Nigeria, etc.).

The Southampton plant assembles various types of domestic appliances, including the famous washing machines on which the firm had based its reputation. The company has also made a name for itself through its liberal labour management policies. Five years ago the British subsidiary dropped the piece-rate system and implemented a complex scheme whereby workers were paid on flat rates plus a productivity bonus calculated on the overall productivity of the plant. In fact the flat rates represented the bulk of the wages and the bonus was just icing on the cake.

As a result the social atmosphere was rather good but productivity had not noticeably increased as the workers could see little relationship between their work and their take-home pay.

However, MWM has the reputation of being a good firm to work for: salaries and wages are decent and, in addition, employees receive various fringe benefits (canteen, social clubs, holiday camps for the children . . .).

3. Exercises

a) *Match the jobs and the different modes of payment*

A	representatives
B	assembly line workers
C	lathe operators
D	lawyers
E	teachers

1	are paid on	flat rates
2	receive	salaries
3	receive	commissions
4	receive	fees
5	are paid on	piece-rates

b) *Complete the following passage using the words below.*

Bill was 55 and was getting increasingly dissatisfied with his job at MWM. Of course the company had dropped _____-_____ after the unions had demanded a more human pay-system. There were also a few _____ to the job, like 20% discounts on MWM machines. But working conditions had not improved dramatically as production rates were still very high. It was indeed very difficult to get a _____. What's more the job was dangerous, but so far the management had always refused to pay _____. He had been injured once and had been on sick-leave for a while, but _____ _____ was not enough to support a family.

He was wondering whether he shouldn't accept the early retirement scheme proposed by the company whereby he would retire at 55 in exchange for a sizeable _____-_____.

After all he could make some more money by doing odd jobs here and there afterwards. Anyway, the company was going through a difficult period and they might very well dismiss him in a few months and then he would only have the _____ to fall back onto.

bonus   danger money   dole   lump sum
perks   piece-rates   sick pay

4. Groupwork

Describe a company. Ideally choose a company you have worked for. Say a few things about its history and describe briefly its activities and pay schemes.

5. Case study: Assembly shop 3

In assembly shop 3 seven workers assemble dish-washing machines. The machines move along on rolling trolleys which each worker pushes to the next position when he or she has finished his or her part of the job.

Each position has been analysed by time and motion study experts and, in theory, they all require the same working time, ten minutes.

In fact, in shop 3 the new worker, Sally Beans, works much faster than her colleagues. She often remains idle as the first three workers don't feed her work fast enough and the other workers cannot keep up with her.

What do you suggest to improve the productivity of shop 3?

↓ Feeder line

1 Jack Snow	2 Dave Martin	3 Andy Green	4 Sally Beans	5 Bert Jones	6 Singh Patel	7 Joe Kirk

quality control ↓

6. The shop stewards meet

Listen to the conversation between two shop stewards, Fred Gibson and Sid Grimley.

Do you understand the management's decision and the workers' reaction?

7. Role play: faction meetings and union–management confrontation

You are going to work in groups of six, three members from management and three from the workers. Your teacher will provide you with role cards which give you information about your role.

Management

Andrew Kershaw, Production Manager
Mike Lawes, Supervisor
Rose Macauley, Personnel Manager

Workers

Fred Gibson, Shop Steward
Sid Grimley, Works Convenor
Jack Snow, worker, Assembly Shop 3

First meet with the other members of your team—management or workers—to prepare your case and decide on your tactics for the joint meeting.

8. Further reading

Tory question on man accused of working too hard

The Opposition will ask the Secretary of State for Employment today to comment on the dismissal of a Luton factory worker after his union had accused him of working too hard.

A spokesman on employment, said yesterday that the case appeared to raise questions about union restrictive practices.

The worker, Mr Neal Daly, a welder, is planning to ask an industrial tribunal to say that he was unfairly dismissed after a series of incidents that started when he exceeded an output figure unofficially set by his colleagues while he was on piecework at the Electrolux factory at Luton. He refused to reduce his work rate and was fined £15 by his union, the Amalgamated Union of Engineering Workers.

He was placed on other work, but appealed to the company, saying he was being victimized.

Mr Arthur Sjogren, a union district secretary, said that Mr Daly had defied a democratic decision in which he took part.

The company denied that Mr Daly had been dismissed for working too hard.

UNIT 11

Wizard Electronics (Marine Department)

This case deals with some of the problems which can arise when a company wants to break into export markets with its products. Wizard Electronics is one such company which is trying to market its marine navigational equipment through overseas agents.

Wizard 2000SN

– FOR EVERYONE WHO NEEDS TO KNOW WHERE THEY'VE BEEN, WHERE THEY ARE AND JUST WHERE THEY'RE GOING.

£1,098*
+ VAT

*UK retail price

The sophisticated answer to navigational requirements. Strong, dependable and very accurate, the yacht navigator comes complete, using log and compass interface, modular construction for ease of servicing and battery back-up for the retention of essential data.

> # EASY BEACON
> ## the last word in RDF
>
> *£350 + VAT*
>
> ●New synthesized Hand-held RDF●Receiver with phase locked loop for sensitive reception of marine and aero beacons ●Internal quartz timing device identifies beacon without reliance on morse code signal ● Push-button selection of frequency synthesized receiver for beacons in the marine band●Padded earpiece headset●Precision prismatic compass●RDF is probably the most effective and widely used navigation facility.
>
> **TRY EASY BEACON AT YOUR DEALERS**
>
> # Wizard Marine
> a member of the WIZARD GROUP   *UK retail price

1. Off to a bad start

Listen to this conversation between the company's Marketing Manager and a young business undergraduate. Make a note of the weaknesses in Wizard Marine's approach to exporting.

2. After office hours

Listen to the two conversations on the tape and then choose the best ending to complete the following sentences.

a) Jenkins   i) was away for the day.
             ii) had gone home.
             iii) was at home.

b) The caller   i) was surprised to hear Jenkins was not in.
                ii) was asked if he wanted to leave a message
                iii) did not wish to leave a message.

c) The office   i) was closed on Monday.
                ii) closed on Fridays.
                iii) no longer belonged to the Wizard group.

d) The message   i) asked Jenkins to call back.
                 ii) informed Jenkins that Guidoni had rung.
                 iii) asked the duty secretary to call on Monday.

e) Jenkins didn't   i) get through to Italy.
                    ii) succeed in speaking to Guidoni.
                    iii) think of leaving a message to be called back.

f) Guidoni   i) was to ring back in the afternoon.
             ii) should have stayed in his office until called.
             iii) didn't tell his secretary he was leaving.

g) Anthony Anderson is furious i) because Guidoni has not called back.
   ii) because he thinks Guidoni is disorganised.
   iii) because he thinks Guidoni is avoiding them.

h) Jenkins i) has never met Guidoni.
   ii) had been impressed by Guidoni's enthusiasm.
   iii) had found Guidoni a bit mysterious.

i) Guidoni i) never sent letters to Wizard.
   ii) sent letters requesting further information.
   iii) sent a single order in three months.

j) Mr Anderson i) wishes to change agents in Italy.
   ii) advises Jenkins to be a bit more careful about whom he appoints.
   iii) would like Jenkins to fly to Italy to visit other agents.

3. Export arrangements

Fill in the gaps in the following passage by using the most suitable words from the list below.

Once a company has decided to _____ their particular _____ of products, the export manager is faced with the ordeal of selecting _____ of distribution abroad. If he decides to use an agent, he may use two types of _____ _____.

The agent may be a distributor who stocks the products which he buys and sells at such a price as enables him to make a profit. This system is obviously attractive for the exporter as he does not need to have capital _____ in stocks abroad and it also guarantees some dedication from the distributor whose own money is involved. A _____ _____ has the exclusive importing rights for a specific territory and a specific product. This type of agreement is especially used for consumer goods: or consumer durables which require locally based after-sales service and are distributed through a variety of retail channels. The drawback is that the distributor has almost the powers of a customer and may resist any change in policy laid down by the exporter.

The second type of agreement uses the services of a _____ _____ who is in charge of promoting products locally, canvassing potential customers and obtaining orders which the _____ will then fulfil for the buyer. This agent will then be paid a commission on the basis of his turnover. Commission _____ vary from 2% to 20% although they may be lower in the case of larger contracts. The amount of work expected from the agent is commensurate with the rate of commission: that is why a _____ is often paid to ensure a minimum income to the agent, especially when he is in charge of a new product.

A _____ agent has exclusive rights over a particular territory and a _____ agent is one who will bear the credit risk for his customers, settling the orders himself in case the buyer defaults.

tied up   export   line   channels   rates   agency agreements   delcredere
principal   sole distributor   commission agent   retainer fee   sole

4. A letter from Italy

The following letter has arrived from Guidoni. Read the letter carefully, then in groups of four discuss whether or not you should take up Guidoni's offer.

SALVIO GUIDONI MOTORSCAFFI
IMPORT-EXPORT MILANO

WIZARD ELECTRONICS
Marine Equipment
Wizard House
16, West Hills Avenue
Croydon
LONDON   CRO 5AB   September 7th, 19

Attention Mr Jenkins

Dear Sirs

We are pleased to inform you that a special exhibition will take place from 20th to 25th October in Torino, the 5th TORINO BOAT SHOW.

In view of the importance of this event for all shipchandlers and boat owners in this country, we wish to reserve a stand in order to promote as efficiently as we can the foreign companies we represent.

However, considering the expense involved, which is considerable as this is a major event, we would appreciate it if you could help us meet this extra cost which will most certainly result in orders for your products.

If you are interested in visiting the show yourself, please let us know sufficiently in advance as accommodation will be rather difficult to find at the last minute.

We look forward to your prompt answer as the matter is quite urgent, the deadline for registration being September 30th.

Yours faithfully

Salvio Guidoni
Managing Director

P.S.: I am very sorry that I missed you when I phoned last week.

5. Answering the letter from Guidoni

You are Simon Jenkins and are to draft the answer to the letter from Italy in accordance with Mr Anderson's instructions in the memo below.

FROM: A.A.
TO: Simon Jenkins
DATE: 12.9.

See letter from Guidoni attached

This is the last straw! Draft a reply for me.
Tell him: a) it's a bit late to warn us at a fortnight's notice.
b) we're very disappointed with this market and his work, and have no intention of investing further capital to help promote other people's products!
c) it's high time he invested in promotion.
d) we are reconsidering our agency agreement with his firm.

AA.

---

6. A meeting with the agents

a) Read the memo from Richard Davies to Simon Jenkins.

FROM: Richard Davies, Trainee

TO: S. Jenkins

DATE: 15th September, 19...

LANGUEDOC NAUTIQUE

As suggested, I have looked into the results of the French market. It would appear that you were right in thinking their results had not been outstanding lately - 3 2000s and 7 RDFs over the last quarter.

A rapid survey of their activity shows

- no advertising in the yachting press
- no network of dealers outside Southwest France
- a price cutting policy has been used without any reference to you

From what I gathered, after a conversation with one of their salesmen, they have arranged for their Sales Manager to come and visit you next week. I checked this and it is indeed true that you are to see a Mr. Serge Camus next Tuesday at 3 p.m.

Attached please find a copy of their contract and the latest statement of commission sent to them.

R.D.

b) You will now be divided into two groups, one from Languedoc Nautique and one from Wizard Marine. Meet in separate groups to prepare this meeting and study the various elements in your file: the contract, the statement of commission and your role cards. You should determine what changes you would like to bring to the situation and be prepared to put your point of view forcibly at the meeting later on.

c) Now, in groups of four, enact the meeting between Wizard and their agents for France. You should discuss: i) the previous results and ii) the changes which you feel should be made concerning the agreement.

WIZARD ELECTRONICS (MARINE DEPARTMENT) LTD

AGENT LANGUEDOC NAUTIQUE AREA FRANCE
       Le Phare d'En Haut   STATEMENT OF COMMISSION No 78
       11430 PORT GRUISSAN DATE 2ND QUARTER 19...

PRODUCT: WIZARD 2000 REF 8945/SAT NAV

date		customer	qty	unit price	value F	commission
APRIL		No invoice recorded				
MAY	16th	ELECTRONIQUE MARINE	5	£880	4.400	110
JUNE	1st	NAUTI CASH	10	£800	8.000	200

PRODUCT: EASY-BEACON REF 6549/RDF

date		customer	qty	unit price	value F	commission
APRIL		No invoice recorded				
MAY	16th	ELECTRONIQUE MARINE	2	£280	560	14
	24th	TOULOUSE YACHTING	4	£280	1120	28
JUNE	1st	NAUTI CASH		£252	2520	63
	8th	ELECTRONIQUE MARINE		£280	840	24

```
                              TOTAL COMMISSION  436
         Expenses for the 1st Quarter [*]       57
     Less Commission on Order no 5678/Dec 18th (23)
         unsettled to date
                                        TOTAL   470
```

Remittance Advice

WIZARD ELECTRONICS LTD
WIZARD HOUSE
16 WEST HILLS AVENUE
CROYDON
ENGLAND
tel: (1502) 774584

LANGUEDOC NAUTIQUE
Le Phare d'En Haut
11430 PORT GRUISSAN
France

Date	Reference	Amount
	AS PER DETAILS ATTACHED	
30.08	015299	£470

Your ref: Our ref: Date:

AGENCY CONTRACT

1 Wizard Electronics (Marine Department) Ltd UK, hereafter called the Principal,
entrust
Languedoc Nautique SARL, Le Phare d'En Haut, PORT GRUISSAN (11430) France, hereafter called the Agent,
with their sole agency for France,
for the sale of the following products:

      EASY-BEACON Radio Direction Finder
           (Patent N^o)
      WIZARD 2000 Satellite Navigator
           (Patent N^o)

2 The Agent will endeavour to serve the interests of the Principal to the best of his ability and provide all information necessary to promote business. He will inform the Principal at once about every order received and follow the latter's instructions as to selling price, terms of payment and delivery.

3 The Agent pledges not to deal in products competing with those referred to in this contract throughout the period of validity of contract and within one full year after cancellation, if any.

4 The Principal will supply the Agent with all necessary advertising material free of charge, duties, and carriage. Two demonstration units shall be sent as soon as they are available but may not be sold and shall be returned by the Agent on request and at the expense of the Principal.

5 The Agent will be supplied with copies of correspondence with firms in his territory and of all invoices resulting from transactions within the said territory.

6 The Agent is not entitled to collect money from customers and may only do so by express authorization.

7 The commission will be 2½% (two and a half percent) of the invoice for all transactions, direct or indirect, carried out with customers within the defined territory.

8 A statement of commission shall be issued quarterly and forwarded to the Agent no later than the end of the following month, and payment falls due on the date the said statement is issued.

9 In the event of a customer defaulting, commission that has already been paid must be repaid and shall be debited to the following statement of commission.

10 Ancillary expenses may be claimed by the Agent only when supported by corresponding itemized receipts and shall not go beyond limits normally accepted in the trade between bona fide business partners.

11 The Agent will inform the Principal of any change in regulations that may influence the position of the products on the market.

12 The contract shall come into force on September 1st, 19. . and is for a period of one year. This Agreement may be terminated by either party giving three months notice by registered letter, and shall be prolonged automatically for a further period of one year provided that notice of termination has not been given within the agreed time.

13 All disputes arising in connection with the present contract will be finally settled under the rules of conciliation of the International Chamber of Commerce by one or more arbitrators appointed according to the said rules.

14 This Agreement cannot be transferred by either party and has been made out in two identical copies, one copy remaining with either party.

Place: CROYDON   Date: August 17th, 19 . .

(Signature of Principal)   (Signature of Agent)

UNIT 12

Carter and Kennedy

M.T. Engineering PLC is a medium-sized company employing 500 people in the Manchester area. It is specialized in the manufacture of highly sophisticated machine-tools for the motor industry. Robert Frost, an engineer, is the founder and majority shareholder of the company.

1. M.T. Engineering: Organisation chart

Fill in the empty boxes with the functions you would expect to find in a company of this sort.

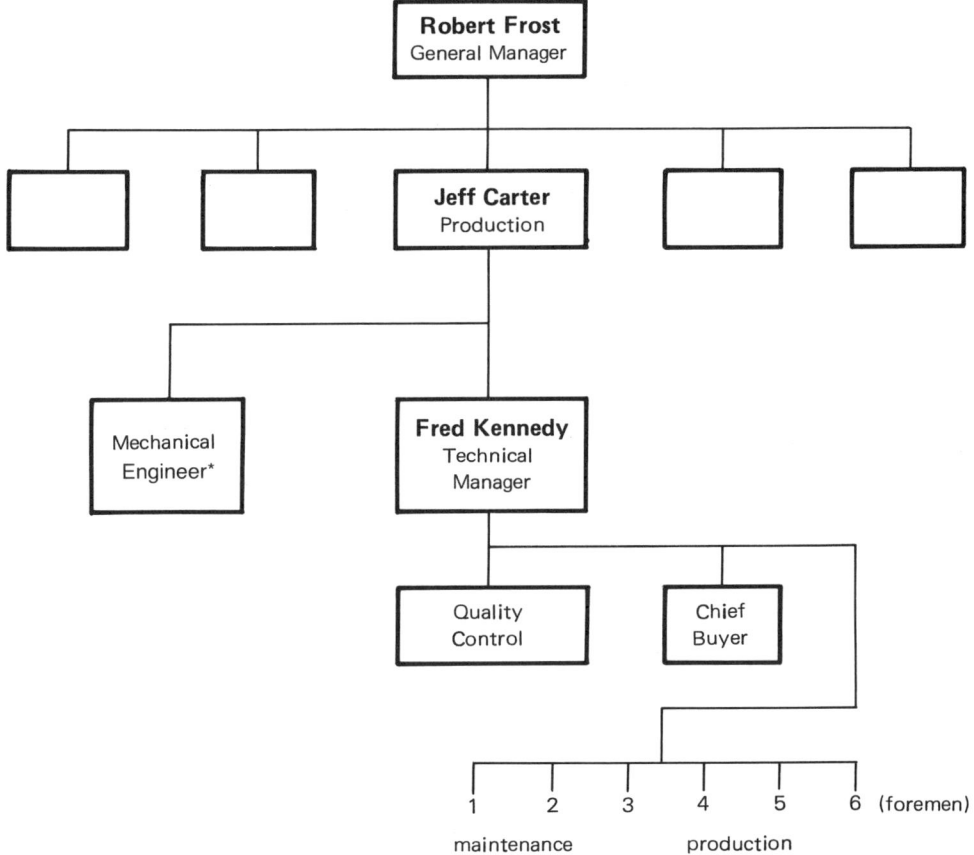

* *Note: Mechanical engineer: he is in charge of designing tools and defining production techniques.*

2. Exercise

Use the correct form of the words from the list below to complete this description of Carter's position in the company.

Jeff Carter who _____ the company 20 years ago was recently _____ to the position of production manager. Now he _____ _____ _____ the whole department and coordinates the work of his four _____ who _____ directly _____ _____ him. His position in the firm is questioned by nobody as he knows the job inside out. He has in fact risen through the ranks, starting as a simple fitter, then becoming foreman, draughtsman, mechanical engineer and technical manager. He himself chose his _____ Fred Kennedy who had been his _____ for 5 years and with whom he had always enjoyed excellent relationships.

to be answerable to ...
to join
deputy
to be responsible for ...
to promote
subordinate
successor

3. Conversation: Robert Frost and Jeff Carter

a) Listen to this conversation between Robert Frost and Jeff Carter. Make a list of the complaints Carter makes about Fred Kennedy. How does Frost defend him?

b) Now use your notes to re-enact the conversation.
Notice the contrast between the two speakers: Frost is cool and rather incredulous; Carter is excited and tends to exaggerate.

Useful phrases

Jeff Carter:
a huge penalty clause
I'm warning you ...
We're heading for trouble if ...

Robert Frost:
This is difficult to believe ...
It isn't as bad as all that, is it?
Leave me a week and I'll come back to you

4. The consultants

Robert Frost had a feeling that there was something else at the back of this tension between Carter and Kennedy and he decided to call in a firm of management consultants and ask them to make a study of the production department with a detailed appraisal of the key-men.

a) *Group work*
Work in groups of three. One is the consultant; the other two are Carter and Kennedy and should use the role cards provided on page 65. The consultant should question the two men and make notes about the following.

	Carter	Kennedy
– age	_____	_____
– education	_____	_____
– joined the company in	_____	_____
– career in the company	_____	_____
	_____	_____
	_____	_____
	_____	_____
	_____	_____
– present job	_____	_____
	_____	_____
– special assignments	_____	_____
	_____	_____
	_____	_____
	_____	_____

Surname: KENNEDY
Name: Frederick
Born: 1940

Education: MA in business studies Manchester University
Joined the company: 1972
Positions held in the company:
- Head of buying   1972–1975
- Head of Quality Control   1976–1978
- Technical Manager   1979

Salary: £20,000 per annum
Assignments:
- overall responsibility for production shops
- allocation of tasks
- fixing rates, working schedules
- responsibility for meeting deadlines
- determining manufacturing processes in association with mechanical engineer

Surname: CARTER
Name: Jeffrey
Born: 1930

Education: apprentice (fitter)
Further education: • draughtsman
                    • mechanical engineer
Joined the company: 1947
Positions held in the company:
- fitter   1947–1950
- foreman   1951–1955
- draughtsman   1956–1960
- mechanical engineer 1961–1962
- technical manager   1962–1979
- production manager   1979

Salary: £30,000 per annum
Assignments:
- overall responsibility for department
- coordinating work of subordinates
- developing manufacturing procedures in relation with R & D
- hiring and firing of direct subordinates
- investments

b) *The consultant's report*

Here are notes made on the two men by one of the consultants. Draft the report for Mr Frost.

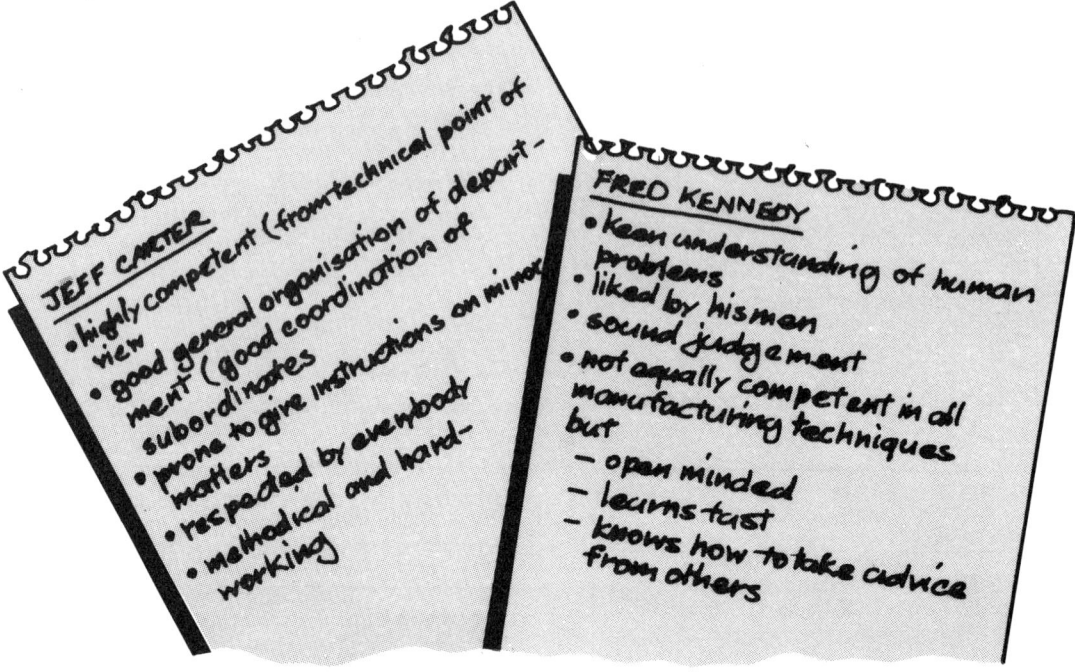

JEFF CARTER
- highly competent (from technical point of view
- good general organisation of department (good coordination of subordinates
- prone to give instructions on minor matters
- respected by everybody
- methodical and hard-working

FRED KENNEDY
- keen understanding of human problems
- liked by his men
- sound judgement
- not equally competent in all manufacturing techniques but
  — open minded
  — learns fast
  — knows how to take advice from others

5. Dialogue

After a preliminary inquiry, Robert Frost was still undecided. He didn't know who was to blame.

Carter was an old friend of his and was respected by everybody in the company.

On the other hand, Kennedy seemed indeed to have the knack for human relations and had shown remarkable organisational abilities in his two previous jobs. This conversation with one of the foremen, Philip Castler, appeared to confirm this impression.

Now listen to the tape again and complete the gapped dialogue below.

Frost: How's your wife Phil?
Castler: ....
Frost: Good, but the poor woman doesn't see much of you these days, you seem to be leaving work later than usual.
Castler: ....
Frost: It doesn't disrupt work does it?
Castler: ....
Frost: He's changed quite a lot of your old ways of doing things hasn't he?
Castler: ....

Repeat the dialogue in pairs. Try to find some alternative expressions for Castler.

6. Case-study

a) How do you explain the tension between the two men? What possible causes are there for the conflict?
b) What solutions would you recommend?

7. Role-Play

Work in groups of three. Frost, the General Manager, receives Jeff Carter and Fred Kennedy in turn and tries to solve the problems.

UNIT 13

Cross-Magill

This case concerns the introduction of a new way of organising work—flexitime—in a pharmaceuticals company. Naturally enough, like anything new, it has its opponents as well as its enthusiasts.

1. The new scheme

Read through the article which appeared in the Cross-Magill house magazine and make sure that you understand the essentials of the new flexitime scheme.

RE~FLEX ACTION?

"About time we had the chance!" "Better late than never!". These are some of the reactions of production workers in Cross-Magill. And what are they so excited about? The answer is Flexitime, on a three-month trial.

Personnel Manager George Sykes is the man behind the scheme. After hearing about the idea for letting workers come and go more freely, he decided to visit Germany to see the system in action. He was so impressed that he persuaded Cross-Magill's management to give it a try. That was 3 years ago and was, as we all know, applied to the office staff only. This experiment was so successful that it was decided at the end of last month to introduce the system on the shop floor for a 3-month trial period. Workers can arrive any time between 8 and 10 and leave any time between 4 and 6; they must be present during the core time of 10-12 and 2-4, and they must do their allotted 40 hours per week average. Calculations are made every week and any credit or debit hours noted.

Despite some earlier scepticism from the unions, all workers say how marvellous it is to be able to come in at 8.30 or even 9.45. "Now we won't have to worry about being late," said one production worker. "And we'll miss all the traffic, just like the office staff", said another, who is looking forward to leaving by 4. "It's good to be treated like responsible adults again!"

Everyone will clock in with a small plastic card (or "key") just like the office staff, and the time worked will be recorded automatically. Employees are allowed a maximum credit or debit of 10 hours which will be carried forward to the next month. Some are already preparing to use a credit of 4 hours to take a half-day off and go fishing!

What about teething problems? "Well, there are bound to be some, just like with the office staff," admits George Sykes, "but we hope they will all be ironed out quickly."

2. Reading comprehension

Read the document below, then answer the questionnaire. The document is an internal company guideline on the operation of flexitime.

CROSS-MAGILL PHARMACEUTICAL PRODUCTS LTD

FLEXITIME OPERATION PROCEDURE

1. The standard daily working hours will be 7 excluding lunch-break (or such variation as is agreed individually in the case of part-time employees or those on a 40 hour week).

2. Except where specially authorised (see 12 below) work shall not commence before 8 a.m. or finish after 7 p.m.

3. Employees (other than part-time employees) must be at work between the hours of 10 a.m. and 12 noon, and 2 p.m. and 4 p.m.

4. The lunch break, to be taken between 12 noon and 2 p.m., must be of a minimum ½ hour duration and may not exceed 2 hours maximum.

5. Starting and finishing times outside the obligatory 4 hours referred to in (3) above are a matter of individual choice, or 'team' agreement where full cover of available working hours is required. In the latter case, the head of department will discuss requirements with those staff affected. For production staff, see 14 below.

6. All workers will clock in with their plastic time card when arriving, and clock out again when leaving. This applies to lunch breaks and tea-breaks as well as the starting and leaving times. Each individual may check his hours worked by inserting his card into the consoles provided.

7. Debit hours accumulated during each calendar month must not exceed 10 hours. Credits or debits up to 10 hours may be transferred to the next calendar month, but are not cumulative.

8. Hours spent on legitimate business purposes away from the normal base must be accounted for, and the reason recorded with the Personnel Dept. The maximum time that may be recorded for absence of a whole day is 7 hours.

9. Absence due to holidays or genuine sickness must be recorded with the Personnel Department.

10. Flexibility of working hours will provide employees with the opportunity of arranging appointments for personal and domestic reasons (visit to dentist or doctor for example, or shopping), in their own time. In exceptional circumstances only will other time off be allowed, and the prior permission of the Head of Department must be obtained so that the hours of absence may be recorded as 'worked' hours.

11. It is not intended that accumulated credit hours be used for the purpose of extending overall holiday entitlement, but with the prior permission of the Head of Department absences for two full days or four half days, not consecutive, may be allowed in any month. This privilege is entirely dependent on the work requirements of the job/department, and there is no appeal against the manager's decision.

12. Flexibility of hours may be suspended at short notice in individual departments on any particular day if essential work demands necessitate such action.

13. These rules may be altered or cancelled at the discretion of management in the light of actual experience of the system, but a minimum of 4 weeks' notice of change will be given.

14. Production teams must fix their starting and leaving times at the beginning of each month, so that production may begin and end regularly each day. These starting and leaving times may be changed at the beginning of a new month, with the prior agreement of the Production Department. These times, once fixed, may not be changed until the end of the month; all members of each team must be present at the times agreed upon. This applies to lunch breaks and any other breaks in production.

Flexitime Questionnaire

1. The longest time anyone could theoretically work in one day is
   a) 9 hours.
   b) 10½ hours.
   c) 11 hours.
   d) no limit.

2. Starting and leaving times for production teams are fixed
   a) by the management.
   b) by the individual.
   c) by each team.
   d) by the shop foreman.

3. The objective of credit hours is
   a) to allow workers to cumulate them to increase their holidays.
   b) to take off two full days or four half days consecutively.
   c) to take off two full days or four half days from time to time, i.e. not consecutively.
   d) to increase their monthly wages.

4. In order to alter or cancel the flexitime system
   a) a company referendum is required.
   b) the management can change it without prior warning.
   c) the management must give 4 weeks notice.
   d) the management must give 4 months notice.

5. The lunch break can last a maximum of
   a) half-an-hour.
   b) an hour.
   c) an hour-and-a-half.
   d) two hours.

6. If a worker wishes to be absent from work during core-hours, he must
   a) ask a friend to put his card in the timing device.
   b) leave his card in the machine overnight.
   c) record the absence with the Personnel Department.
   d) tell his foreman the next day.

7. The maximum number of hours credit or debit you may accumulate is
   a) no limit.
   b) 10 hours a week.
   c) 10 hours a month.
   d) 100 hours a year.

8. The length of the core time which must be worked by everyone is
   a) 4 hours.
   b) 6 hours.
   c) 5 hours.
   d) 3 hours.

9. If you wish to check the number of hours worked
   a) you must go to the Personnel Department.
   b) you can put your card into a special console.
   c) there is no way of knowing before the end of each week.
   d) you fill in a special form.

3. Background information

Here is part of a discussion between George Sykes and Peter Russell, Cross-Magill's Chief Production Engineer. Make a careful note of what they say: you will need your notes later in order to prepare Sykes' report.

4. Management report

Head Office has asked George Sykes to prepare a report on how well/badly flexitime has worked during the first four weeks of its application to production staff. Using the information you have gathered from Peter Russell and George Sykes, draw up a short preliminary draft report outlining the situation so far. It should also give details of how you expect the system will operate in the future, and you may make any recommendations you wish.

5. Pair-work

Listen to the dialogue between Sykes and Alan Riley, one of the shop-stewards in the production department.
   When you have heard the recording, and using the notes below, re-enact the discussion.

Sykes is looking for more information and generally testing the union's reactions and the workers' feelings. Where necessary, he is prepared to correct Riley's statements and accept a possible compromise.

Riley is enthusiastic about the effects of introducing flexitime, and gives his and the workers' reasons. However, he points out drawbacks and offers a possible solution.

Here are some expressions you can use:

Look
Listen

I'd like to know . . .
Hang on (a minute)
Wait
What about . . .
How about . . .
Tell me, . . .

To be honest, . . .
Frankly,
By the way
Incidentally
For a start, . . .

Of course
Actually
In fact, . . .

6. Groupwork

Work in groups of three or four. Look closely at this copy of the memorandum George Sykes prepared on the application of flexitime to production staff. It was drawn up with the help of the Production Department.

In your group try to decide what effects flexitime has had on production and costs.

Memorandum

FROM   :   Personnel Manager

TO   :   All Works Committee Members

DATE   :   10 March 19..

RE :   Flexible working hours :   production staff

Below is an updated appraisal of the implementation of flexible working hours in the production departments. The details concern the first eight weeks of this year. May I remind you that the trial period still has some two months to run; no definitive conclusions should therefore be drawn on the basis of this information.

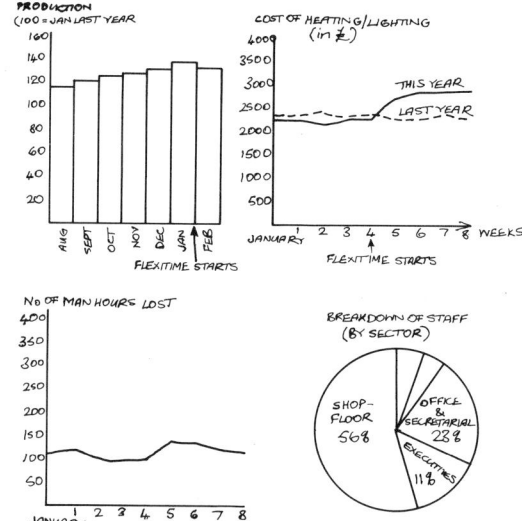

In evaluating the graphs above, a number of points should be borne in mind. Whilst overall productivity has fallen, this is not always the case in every single shop. Similarly, the increase in overheads has to be seen in the context of a particularly cold spell of weather at the end of January. As for man-hours lost, despite a sudden rise with the introduction of flexitime, the trend is now clearly downwards. A breakdown of staff by sector has been added, for purposes of comparison.

GS

7. Role play: The Works' Committee Meeting

The meeting has been called exceptionally, to discuss the ways in which flexitime has proved of value or otherwise for production. Everyone can express his or her views freely. Some problems will have to be solved, but this should be done, insofar as is possible, by mutual agreement. As a committee, you may of course recommend withdrawing the system if you feel it is not working.

The following people are present:

George SYKES, Personnel Manager (in the chair)
Peter RUSSELL, Chief Production Engineer
Jan SIMMONS, Catering Staff Representative
Alan RILEY, shop-steward (APS: Association of Pharmaceutical Staffs)
Martin NEWCOMBE, Company Secretary
Ralph COOKE, representing the Union of Managerial Employees.

UNIT 14

Zilvanium

This case is in seven stages and looks at issues raised by co-operation between multinationals and Third World countries. Each stage covers a particular area of business and contains factual information which builds up to a final negotiating session.

Stage I   THE STOCK EXCHANGE

1. Investment advice

Work in pairs, one of you as a small investor, the other as a stock broker.

Investor   Your portfolio includes

Oils	20 BP and 5 Shell
Breweries	8 Bass
Foods	7 Sainsbury

Phone your broker for a report on today's session, then seek his advice.

Broker   Today's market report (extract)

Oils	BP	420p, down 5p
	Shell	360p, down 5p
Breweries	Bass	235p, up 4p
Foods	Sainsbury	615p, down 20p

Give today's results to your client and offer him your advice.

2. Stock Exchange report

Look up a London Stock Exchange report in a paper and make up a commentary of your own to describe the situation briefly. Note the words and phrases commonly used and try to include them in your commentary.

3. Financial report, Best Radio

a) Read the following extract from the financial press and note the style of English used.

> **Eventful week ends with a firm note**
>
> The London Stock Exchange ended an eventful week on a quietly firm note with most sections displaying a preponderance of plus signs.
>
> Breweries did well, encouraged by the 5.8 per cent rise in beer production during March. Bass made one of the best rises 4p higher at 235p.
>
> Foods in contrast provided a dull corner. Suggestions that a new price-cutting war may soon break out brought sharp falls to the High Street supermarket giants. J. Sainsbury which earlier in the week reported bumper earnings took a 25p tumble at 610p. Tesco ended up 3p at 56p.

b) Prepare a Stock Exchange report for the finance programme on Best Radio. Use the data provided to make your report and comment on the movements in the share market. Some useful expressions to account for variations are given below.

```
Data:
British Funds                    Insurance
   3p 1984   85¾....+¼               Sun Al & L  804....-2

Banks and Discount Houses        South African Mines
   Lloyds     406....+10             Welkom     725....-15
   Nat West   420....+2
                                 Mining
Commerce and Industry               Rio Tinto Zinc  444....+5
   Boots     231....+4
   ICL        57......+3          Shipping
                                     P & O      152....+8
Oil
   Burmah    146....+3
```

Useful phrases

To account for downward movement
As a result of rumours of ...
Following speculation about ...
Owing to pressure from ...

To account for upward movement
After / *Following* { *the announcement of ...* / *the acquisition of ...* / *hints of a record dividend ...* }

To predict movement
The downward/upward trend is (not) likely/expected to continue ...

📻 4. Radio report

Listen to this radio broadcast on Best Radio, 234 m MW and then answer the following questionnaire.
a) This was the financial report.
       stock exchange report.
b) Zilvanium is a successful company.
       an electronic battery.
       a new metal.
c) Indian Ocean Holdings shares have been rising
       on the London Metal Exchange for 4 days.
       on the London Stock Exchange for 4 days.
       on the London Stock Exchange for five days.
d) At the close of business, Indian Ocean Holdings share value
       had dropped sharply.
       had fallen slightly.
       had risen again.
e) The Cathode Zilvanium Mining Company
       is owned by the Federation of Anodins government.
       is backed by opposition minorities.
       is a mining subsidiary of IOH.

5. A note on the LME

The London Metal Exchange, which is part of the commodity market in London, has been situated in Whittington Avenue since 1882, and consists of two sets of sessions commencing at 12 a.m. and two more commencing at 3.45 each day. Dealings in metals are for cash or for any market day up to 3 months forward, mainly in 3 months futures. An official price is agreed by a fixing committee on the basis of the day's trading for both cash and futures and it is accepted throughout the world.

Stage II MINING

1. Pairwork

You are going to work in pairs with a colleague.
Student B Turn to the next page
Student A Read only the information on this page and then summarize it for your colleague. Your colleague may want to ask you some questions about your information.

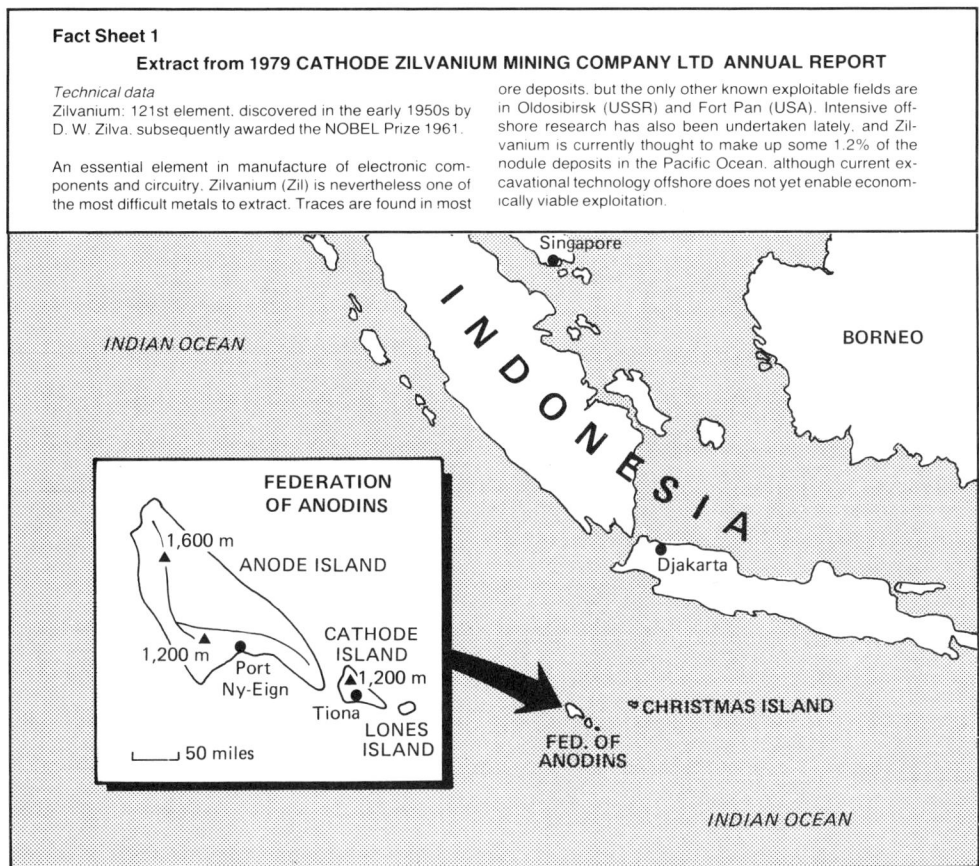

Fact Sheet 1
Extract from 1979 CATHODE ZILVANIUM MINING COMPANY LTD ANNUAL REPORT

Technical data
Zilvanium: 121st element, discovered in the early 1950s by D. W. Zilva, subsequently awarded the NOBEL Prize 1961.

An essential element in manufacture of electronic components and circuitry, Zilvanium (Zil) is nevertheless one of the most difficult metals to extract. Traces are found in most ore deposits. but the only other known exploitable fields are in Oldosibirsk (USSR) and Fort Pan (USA). Intensive offshore research has also been undertaken lately, and Zilvanium is currently thought to make up some 1.2% of the nodule deposits in the Pacific Ocean, although current excavational technology offshore does not yet enable economically viable exploitation.

Your colleague also has some important information about Zilvanium mining and you should try to find out from him:
i) the location of the Zilvanium mine;
ii) the conditions under which mining takes place;
iii) the content of Zilvanium per tonne of ore.

Also check the following information which you have been given:
iv) the mine is rumoured to contain ten more years of commercially exploitable ore;
v) transportation is easy thanks to excellent river facilities nearby.

Student B Read only the information on this page and then summarize it for your colleague. Your colleague may want to ask you some questions about your information.

Fact Sheet 2

The Tiona Heights Mine (Cathode Island, Federation of Anodins)

The Cathode Zilvanium deposits, discovered during preliminary exploration in 1966, were initially believed to be limited in extent; recent excavation has shown that the deposit is more extensive than initially believed and that exploitation may continue steadily for at least two decades while there is still no alternative supply available in the world on a competitive basis.

The Tiona Heights mine is located 10 miles inland, in a mountainous region of thick rain-forest vegetation. Rainfall currently averages 240 inches per year, often occurring in downpours of 10 inches within an hour. This can make mining and transportation dangerous and hazardous. Exceeding 80 million tons, the ore body averages 0.24% Zilvanium per tonne of ore. There is now some evidence that additional commercial grade mineralisation exists beyond the limits of the proven reserves. Mine life is now believed to be around 20 years at current production rate.

THE TIONA HEIGHTS MINE

Cathode Island, Federation of Anodins

Your colleague also has some important information about Zilvanium mining and you should try to find out from him:
  i) the location of the Federation of Anodins;
 ii) the uses of Zilvanium in industry;
iii) whether exploitable deposits exist elsewhere.

Check the following information which you have also heard:
 iv) offshore research has proved very promising;
  v) the exploitation of offshore deposits will commence very soon.

2. The refining process

Look at the diagram and then complete the description of the refining process using the correct form of the verbs given.

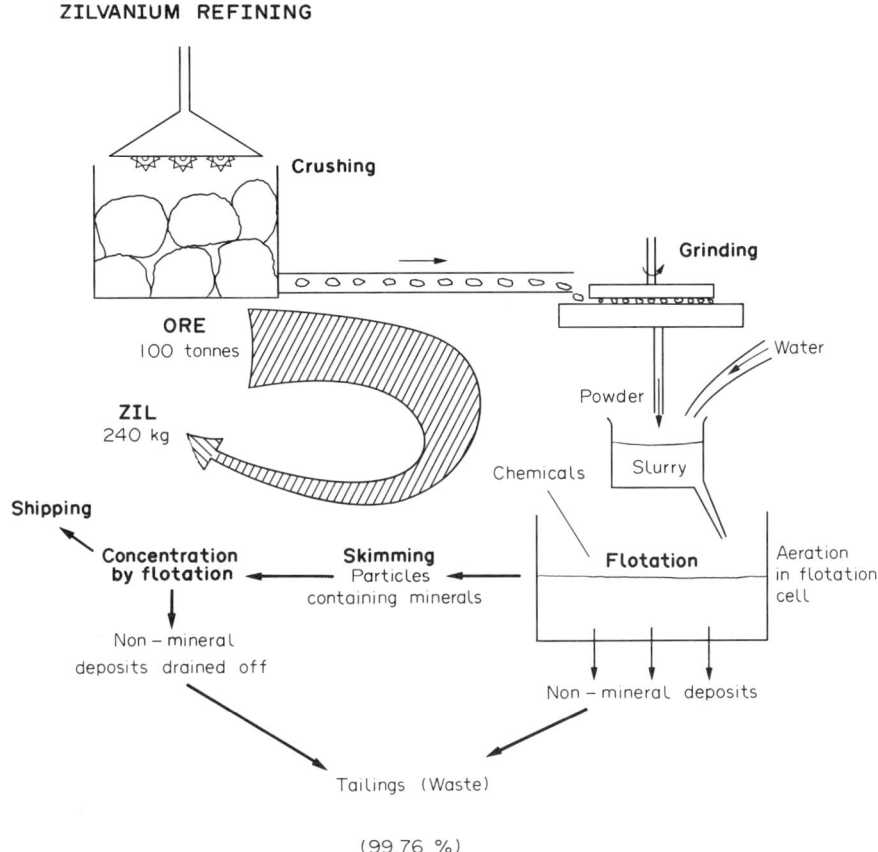

ZILVANIUM REFINING

The ore is first _____ into small gravel-sized pieces. It is then _____ to a powder to which water is _____ to form a slurry. This is then mixed with various chemicals and _____ in open-air tanks. Mineral-containing deposits _____ to the top and are _____ off. Poorly mineralised and non-mineral particles _____ to the bottom and are _____ off for disposal as tailings. This waste, which could otherwise create mountainous and occasionally dangerous heaps is _____ into nearby rivers and _____ to the sea.

add   aerate   crush   drain   dump   float   grind   sink   skim   wash

3. Presentation

Using a simple set of graphs and charts explain the Zilvanium refining process, highlighting the main facts about the 'wonder metal' from the point of view of
a) a local ecologist movement
b) a development manager in favour of further investment.

Stage III FINANCIAL ASPECTS

1. Number crunching: teamwork

MEMO

FROM: Chairman
TO: Financial Director
DATE: March 12th, 19...

Cathode Zilvanium Mining Company

As I am being interviewed on a London TV network next Friday please provide me with the latest data available, indicating which points are sensitive, and giving hints for non-committal statements to be used on this occasion.

T.B.J.

Look at the information provided below and fill in any figures which are missing. Then draft a carefully worded memo in reply to the Chairman, providing him with all the information you feel he may need to counter the questions of the television journalists.

OWNERSHIP AND CAPITAL STRUCTURE OF THE CATHODE ZILVANIUM MINING COMPANY LTD.

Fed. of Anodins	I.O.H.	Public
20%	54%	26%

Equity capital: 287,375,000 shares
at £1 per share
58,234 shareholders listed
8,164 Anodin residents

The 23 largest shareholders account for 78.67% of the equity.

From the data provided, calculate the **total** Anodin direct income derived from the mining activity.

2. On the air: simulation

In teams devise a two minute story for British Business News, entitled *Spotlight on Zilvanium* based on this Reuter Newsflash:

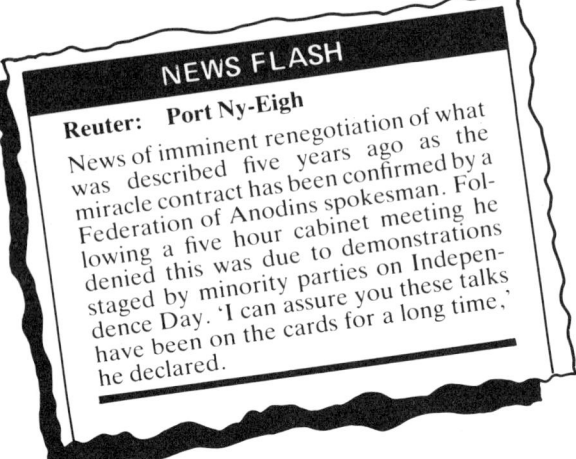

Your story line should include:
    the rumours
    what Zilvanium is: data
    financial aspects
    forecast on the outcome of current moves.

3. Review

Write a short TV criticism or review of the programmes presented by other teams.

Stage IV CONTRACTS

1. The Zilvanium agreement (signed 5 years ago)

Principal terms of the Cathode Zilvanium Mining Company Agreement of December 19... and applicable Anodin Tax Law

Royalty: 1.25% of net revenue
Income tax:
1) Tax holiday (zero tax rate) for 5 years beginning year of the Agreement.
2) Tax rate of 25% beginning in year 6 of the Agreement and rising by 5% steps to 50% in year 11 and continuing at that rate through to year 28.
3) Tax rate escalation of 1% per year beginning in year 29 and rising to a maximum rate of 66%.
4) Accelerated depreciation: capital expenditures may be written off against income as rapidly as desired after the tax holiday ends.

5) 20% of net income may be excluded from calculations for tax purposes.

   Government ownership: The Federation of Anodins is allowed to purchase at par up to 20% of the shares issued.

   Infrastructure: The Federation of Anodins is obliged to construct at its own expense all public facilities not directly associated with the mining operations.

   Term: 25 years, renewable for successive 15-year terms at the company's option, with modifications only to royalty and rents in the first and second such renewals.

2. Comparing contracts

Now compare the terms of the Zilvanium Agreement with those of other mining concessions outlined in the table below.

Useful phrases

     provides
The Agreement makes provision for . . .
     makes no provision

There is no mention of . . . in the Zilvanium Agreement.

A major point of the contract is . . .

Major terms of mining concessions in other countries

	Country A Copper, gold, silver	Country B Sulphur	Country C Zinc
Income tax	35% in first ten years, 42% thereafter	35% in years 4–11, 7% thereafter	22.5%
Tax holiday	None	3 years	None
Royalties	Copper 3.6% Gold and silver 1%	None	None
Participation by host country	Equity available at 2% p.a. up to 20%	None	51% equity to be paid for out of future dividends
Other taxes	None	Minimum tax of 5% net revenue in years 4–11, 10% thereafter	Minerals tax of 51% of net profits before income tax
Tax credits and depreciation	8% investment tax credit up to 50% of tax payable; depreciation up to 12½% p.a., straightline	Depreciation at up to 12½% p.a., postponable until year 4	None
Transactions with affiliated companies	Limitation on interest payments to affiliates	Interests paid to affiliates must be approved by Ministry of Finance; technical fees not deductible	Limitation on management and sales fees payable to affiliates
Duration	30 years	30 years	25 years

3. Written Follow-up

Write a memo pointing out similarities and differences between the various contracts. In conclusion pass a judgement on whether or not the Zilvanium Agreement was favourable to the company.

4. Research

Find out something about a real life mining operation and prepare to make a presentation to the class.

5. Political broadsheet

WORDS ARE NOT ENOUGH

Five years ago, the Cathode Zilvanium Mining Company began open excavations for Zilvanium in our island province of Cathode. The terms of their activities were set by the Government on behalf of the nation but without special consultation with the people of Cathode. The terms are set down in the 19   Mineral Agreement, passed by Parliament in 19   . They are an insult to our people.

Social disruption
All areas affected by the excavation have been thrown into chaos.
The Government's attempt at compromise, by selling mineral rights without selling the land, is unsatisfactory: land is rendered useless by waste, and its contents are exploited without proper reward for its owner. Royalties to landowners must be increased immediately.

Dispossession of land is not the only problem. Local inhabitants are recruited for work at the mines at contemptible wages in view of the wealth extracted by the Company. Local crafts and traditions are dying, foreign customs are creating ill feeling in this area. The Company's so-called "social investments" are limited to providing access-roads to its own sites, and minimal social and housing facilities for its own employees.
Our people must live in happiness, not in misery.

Ecological disruption
Excavation areas and adjacent waste-heaps are left useless for traditional agricultural and spread pollution. Dust, and fumes, and smoke from excavation sites, processing and digging are harmful to local wildlife and to adjacent agricultural land. Enclosure of land prevents free movement of wildlife. Permanent concrete structures will prevent use of the land after the exploitation for minerals. The sacred land of our fathers is being desecrated before our very eyes.

Economic disruption
The vast profits from such activity are not invested locally by the Company, but overseas. The Government has granted terms which insult our island: a low tax-levy, an extended "tax-holiday", inadequate royalties for land-owners, inadequate social investment and compensation . . . New negotiations must redress the balance in our favour. Moreover, the new terms must be imposed on the Sahdu Zinc Mining Company, whose excavations in the North, due to begin in 198., will otherwise be as shameful to our country as the existing ones.

Political consequences
Popular enthusiasm for the Wimto Party among the people of Cathode province is growing daily, and we are receiving political and financial backing from all other areas of the island. Only the Wimto Party can guarantee action against foreign domination and vested interest within this Anode-dominated Government. A majority situation will shortly enable the Party to bring down the Government and to impose Cathodian dominance over the exploiters of our island's national wealth. Extreme injustice calls for extreme remedies.

Help save our island! Down with Anodin domination!

Stage V POLITICS

1. Question Time

Back in the Federation of Anodins things are becoming uncomfortable for the Government.

Listen to the recording of Question Time in Parliament and say whether the following are true or false.

a) These speeches are made on the occasion of the Anniversary of Independence.
b) The Wimto Party would like to oust foreign investors.
c) They accuse the present government of selling out the Cathode people's interests.
d) There is a threat of violent action if nothing is done to improve the situation.
e) The Prime Minister addressed himself to the Leader of the Wimto Party.
f) The Prime Minister denied there were any discussions on the contract.
g) The Prime Minister didn't comment on the subversive tone.
h) The Wimto Party leader pointed out the detrimental effects of mining on the islanders' lives.

2. Research Work

If you can, listen to the BBC programme 'Today in Parliament'. Make a note of the way political leaders deal with unexpected questions.

3. Debate

In two groups prepare to debate the following topics. One group should propose the subject and the other oppose it strongly.

a) Nuclear power represents the only viable power source for the future.
b) The occasional coastline disaster is a small price to pay for the benefits derived from bigger oil tankers.

4. Further reading

Slicing the cake

Port Ny-Eigh

Who is to get Cathode's Zilvanium wealth? Indian Holdings Ltd's original concession for the Cathode zilvanium mine was negotiated by the colonial rulers just before the independence of the Federation of Anodins. Thanks to zilvanium price boom, and because the mine proved a much bigger operation than originally foreseen, it provided half of IOH's shareholders' income. Predictably, once the Federation achieved internal self-government, the new government initiated discreet moves to find a way to a new contract that should be agreed before the end of the first five year period of activity which happens to be the end of this year. Most Anodin officials feel that the new contract should bring an immediate increase in income tax, instead of a gradual rise over a long period. Profits equal to those of last year—a good year—would give the Anodin government substantial income tax receipts on top of its royalty income and the £4.3 million levied on outgoing dividends.

This huge prospective influx of zilvanium wealth has inflamed local jealousies. And what Katanga once was to the ex-Belgian Congo, Cathode Island could now become for the Anodins. It is an island which lies 35 miles West of the capital, Port Ny-Eigh. Its 5,600 inhabitants are moving towards a provincial government of their own. And they too have their eyes on the zilvanium revenue. Early this month, a local party issued an ultimatum to the Federation government that they would cut off the mine's water supply unless it was agreed that the zilvanium royalties be shared more fairly with the island. The Anodin chief minister, Mr Nirella, is believed to be ready to consider this demand. But even if he does, nobody believes the Cathodians will be content for long. The people of the Federation have precious little feeling of national unity anyway and most regions want more local autonomy. The Cathodians may not be content until they have their hands on the entire mine revenues, which would give them an annual per capita income higher than that of Kuwait. Meanwhile IOH is caught in the crossfire.

Stage VI PUBLIC RELATIONS

1. Press releases

Read the following press releases issued in response to the debate about the Zilvanium mining contract.

15th March 19

Following recent public concern over the existing agreement with the Cathode Zilvanium Mining Company Ltd, a spokesman at Government House today issued the following statement:

The Elected Government of the Federation of the Anodins notes with some concern the popular speculation and alarm prompted by recent Parliamentary discussion. Matters concerning the terms of mineral rights and foreign companies are currently under consideration, and the Administration cannot approve independent initiatives intended to hasten its present examination of this question.

Press release issued by the Cathode Zilvanium Mining Company Ltd at 10 p.m. in answer to local pressure over their mining activities at Tiona Heights:

16th March 19

As guests of the people of the Federation of the Anodins, the Company would like to express its regret for the ill-feeling which has recently been voiced concerning its excavation activities. The Company would remind those concerned that its activities are in accordance with the terms agreed with the People's Government of the Federation of the Anodins in December 19 , and that these terms have been strictly adhered to in its activities.

However, the Company is eager to maintain its good relations with its island hosts and would urge employees and neighbours to feel free to contact the Information Department over any matter of concern, and would be willing to engage in dialogue with any representative group with possible grievances.

Note that in press statements of this kind
a) only the third person is used—'the Government . . . notes . . .'
b) 'would' is frequently used for emphasis—'The Company would remind those concerned . . .'

2. Drafting a statement

Read the following article about a disturbance at the Company's Head Office and then draft press statements:
a) on behalf of the company, expressing its concern about the incident;
b) on behalf of the Wimto Party.

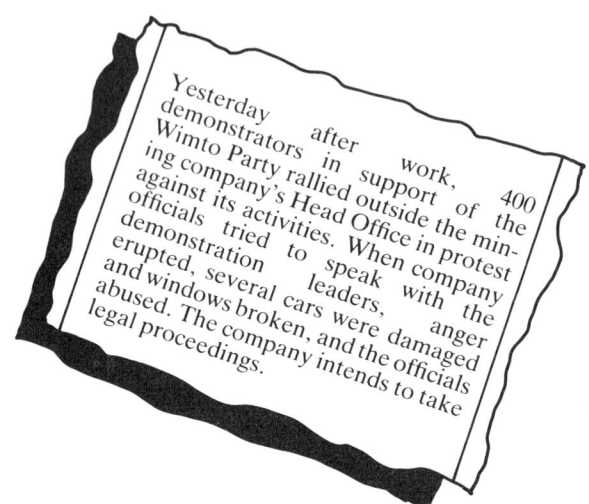

Yesterday after work, 400 demonstrators in support of the Wimto Party rallied outside the mining company's Head Office in protest against its activities. When company officials tried to speak with the demonstration leaders, anger erupted, several cars were damaged and windows broken, and the officials abused. The company intends to take legal proceedings.

3. Telephone conversation: role play

John Spear, Managing Director of Cathode Zilvanium Mining Company, calls Terence Jay, Chairman of IOH, at IOH Headquarters in London.

Work in pairs. Choose your roles, read the role information below and act out the telephone conversation.

John Spear
Prepare some notes to ring up IOH Headquarters in order to point out the urgency of sending negotiators to help local executives.

a) The negotiation is becoming a political issue that seems to be getting out of hand. Delaying tactics, which had been the instructions from London, are no longer applicable.
b) Other parties (countries and multinationals) are showing an interest in the possibility of interfering.
c) Delaying the talks any further might threaten the very presence of the company in the islands.

Terence Jay
You are quite satisfied with the financial performance of the Mining Company. As the agreement with the Federation of Anodins was signed four years ago, there is still another year to run without any tax to pay. This subsidiary accounts for half the dividend declared by IOH this year, so you do not wish to change the state of things. Try to calm down your subordinate.

Stage VII NEGOTIATING

1. Faction meetings

You are going to work in two groups with an independent mediator:

        Company negotiators   Anodin Government Negotiators
                      \   /
                   Independent Mediator

You each have a file of confidential information which you should study carefully in your groups before the negotiation session begins.
    You should also appoint a head of your negotiating team and decide on the roles of the other members of your group.
    When you have studied your file, prepare an agenda which your group would like to see for the meeting which is to follow.

2. Agreeing on the agenda

The two delegation heads should meet, each accompanied by an assistant, to agree on the agenda for the meeting. The independent mediator will chair the meeting.

3. The negotiation

The two parties now meet to discuss the points on the agenda. Each party should choose its own secretary to be in charge of drafting minutes on the items agreed in the meeting.

The meeting will be chaired by the mediator and either party may ask for the meeting to be adjourned for private consultation at any time.

Government Negotiators   FEDERATION OF ANODINS

EXHIBIT A

Confidential report on the situation on Cathode Island

Although there has not so far been much response from Cathodians to the Wimto Party's main line of 'Zilvanium profits to Cathode Islanders only', most people on the Island agree that the government has not devoted enough attention and investment to the island whose inhabitants suffer from the drawbacks of the mining activity. More investment in social facilities and compensation for damage to ancestral land should be made *and* publicised. As the company is the main employer on the island, little demonstration has been organised so far to put forward local claims for fear of retaliation on individuals. In this respect, the government of the Federation is perceived as being in the hands of the company and little hope or faith is put in its ability to improve the fate of the island. Hence the growing sympathy for Wimto Party break away line.

EXHIBIT B

Investment by other multinational companies currently being considered at government level

1. River Ghil dam: a £7,900,000 project to be financed with the help of international banking institutions provided there is enough evidence of political stability and long-term revenue.
2. A £3 million container terminal to be financed and run by a pool of shipping companies in Port Ny-Eigh new docks.
3. United Vitamins has offered to finance a vast agricultural development plant to start a citrus fruit processing industry, the Anodin government supplying the labour and the land.
4. A uranium mine is to be opened in the northern hills of Anode Island and another major deposit might well be found on the corresponding ridge on Cathode Island.

EXHIBIT C

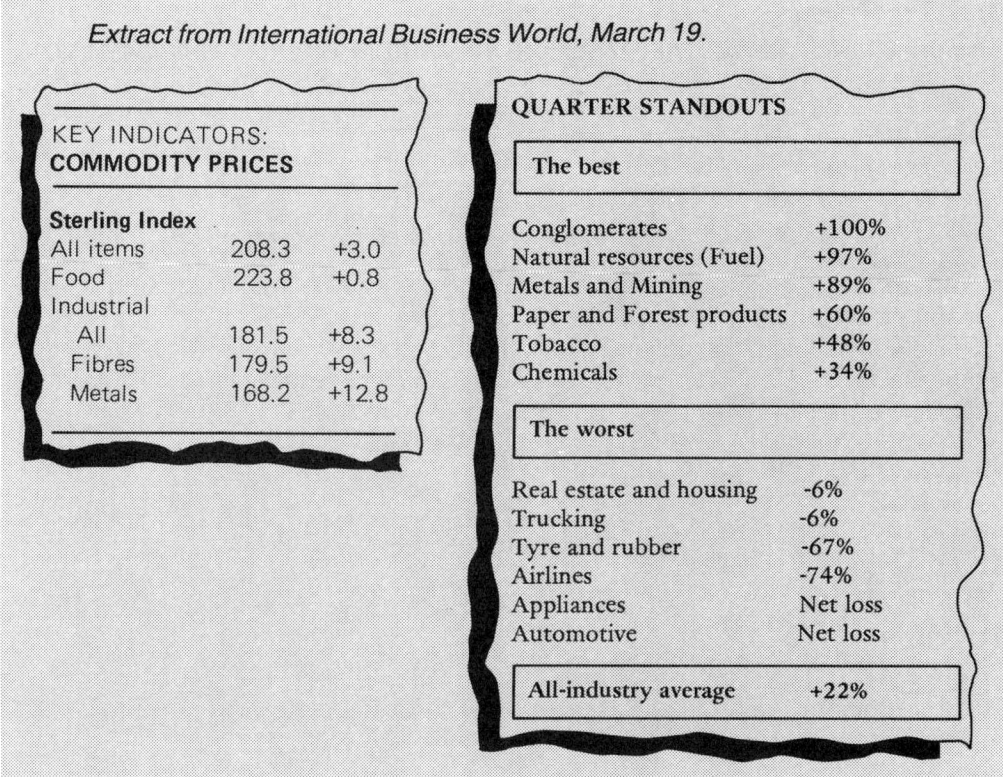

Extract from International Business World, March 19.

KEY INDICATORS:
COMMODITY PRICES

Sterling Index
All items	208.3	+3.0
Food	223.8	+0.8
Industrial		
All	181.5	+8.3
Fibres	179.5	+9.1
Metals	168.2	+12.8

QUARTER STANDOUTS

The best	
Conglomerates	+100%
Natural resources (Fuel)	+97%
Metals and Mining	+89%
Paper and Forest products	+60%
Tobacco	+48%
Chemicals	+34%

The worst	
Real estate and housing	-6%
Trucking	-6%
Tyre and rubber	-67%
Airlines	-74%
Appliances	Net loss
Automotive	Net loss

All-industry average	+22%

EXHIBIT D

Main recommendations to Developing Countries when negotiating a mining contract with the Mining subsidiary of a foreign firm
by John Adler Seel, Professor of Macroeconomics at Harvard

1. In view of the heavy investment and the high-risk involved companies should be granted EITHER a tax-holiday OR accelerated depreciation, but these two concessions should not be combined.
2. Governments should avoid taking out loans to buy their shares of the equity. The latter should be paid on future dividends.
3. Companies should undertake by contract to increase their social contribution: housing, services, infrastructure. A detailed schedule should be determined in advance and easy control provided for.
4. In case of unforeseen rises in world metal prices, the government should receive a share of the increase in profit.
5. Landowners should receive royalties for the use of their land by the companies proportionate to production, and not a fixed sum.
6. There should be greater training and employment opportunities for local people, i.e. accelerated indigenization.
7. Whenever practicable, development of local processing industries should be provided for.

RESTRICTED

Company Negotiators   THE CATHODE ZILVANIUM MINING COMPANY LTD
A subsidiary of Indian Ocean Holdings Ltd

EXHIBIT A

Report on contacts with Wimto Party Deputy Executive Secretary

Intense, ascetic figure who appears to fear the dominating influence of the central government as much as that of foreign capital.

Determined to take advantage of the renegotiation to push his party's secession line if effects on Cathode islanders not tangible enough. More sensitive to visible effects on life in the island than revenue.

Leads a handful of noisy members in the National Assembly.

EXHIBIT B

Extract from Professor Adler-Seel's article in '*Third World Today*'.

In view of the heavy investment and the high-risk involved companies should be granted EITHER a tax-holiday OR accelerated depreciation, but these two concessions should not be combined.

delenit aigue duos dolore et molestias excepturi sint occaecat cupiditat non provident tempor... in culpa qui officia deserunt mollit anium il... be dolo. fuga. Et har und... facilis est... expedit distinct. Nam... tempe soluta nobis... option... que nihil impedit d...ming id quod m... facer p...sim omnis... ...mmenda... omnis rep...

There should be greater training and employment opportunities for local people, i.e. accelerated indigenization.

f... ...ff... ... ...ig... ...itional notione... offic... et oper... ...for... ... ...ralitat magis conveniunt, da but ...tung benevolent sub conediant, et apt ex ad quiet. finibus caritat praesari con...ening nulli sit amet pro... ...quas indigen... ...bi... a natura proficis va...le sapient sine nulla inuria autend inanc is p...i... ...i... ...i... ...iderabile. Concupis plusque in ipsinuria detri ... ...i... ...it... ...u... ...enectmen... ...arum inian. Itaque... ... 'tilid' de... rec

Whenever practicable, development of local processing industries should be provided for.

EXHIBIT C

Conclusions of IOH think tank in London

RESTRICTED

Effect on company of possible concessions

1. *Removal of tax holiday:* reduction of declared profits (to £24,914,000, based on 19.. profits)
   Abandon accelerated depreciation: will tend to increase *declared*-profits by approx. £25,000,000 in first year, decreasing thereafter. So more tax benefit for Anodin Government.
2. *Government shares paid for by future dividends:* Additional loans needed, as government shares not paid-up until dividends declared. A short-term interest liability.
3. *Greater social contribution:* Non-productive costs, not tax allowable. Negotiation should revolve around the time table and the size of such contribution.
4. *Government share in unforeseen rise in metal prices:* The possibility of a rise in world metal prices was a decisive factor in setting up the whole venture. This is the least acceptable Government proposal as increased prices would anyway lead to increased profits and corresponding taxes.
5. *Royalties to landowners:* Leads to direct increase of costs, dependent on quantity mined.
6. *Indigenization:* Not practicable in specialist technical and managerial areas, at least initially. Will be difficult to refuse when higher education is more developed in the country: would then lead to a take-over by the host country.
7. *Developing local processing industries:* Only interesting if such industries owned by same shareholders, with similar initial financing. Would however confront Indian Ocean Holdings with the problem of marketing finished products, which is not a diversification contemplated at the moment. It has up to now been the policy of IOH to enter into long-term agreements with smelting and refining companies in industrialised countries in order to avoid the risks involved in the marketing of finished products.

UNIT 15

The Daltons

This case centres on financial problems and is divided into three separate parts.

Part I

1. 75,000 sweatshirt deal

Russian order for transfers: £150,000 deal boosts company

The transfer market in Braintree is booming because of a £150,000 contract from Russia.

Lucky Luck, which has been around for twenty years and now exports to 100 different countries, has just picked up its largest order ever—for more than 75,000 transfers.

Managing Director, Bert Dalton went to a trade show in Moscow 18 months ago and reckons the response from the public was "staggering".

After a meeting with the Russians in June, he accepted the £150,000 offer and is now taking on 10 school-leavers to boost his 36-strong staff.

Lucky Luck is based on the Broomhills industrial estate and its previous biggest contract was £45 000 from Yugoslavia.

It manufactures iron-on transfers and plans to import and market the machines for putting them on T-shirts and other clothes.

Mr Dalton said yesterday: "We are the only company outside the United States that produces the glitter-type transfers. Two-thirds of our transfers go overseas and I did 32 shows last year. But this is definitely a big breakthrough for the company."

28th March

2. A radio news item

Listen to the recording of the radio news item and summarize what you hear.

3. Reconstructing the balance sheet

A financial consultant has been asked for his opinion of the company's position. Listen to his telephoned reply and reconstruct the balance sheet from the information given.

Liabilities	Assets

4. Studying the accounts

Examine the accounts below and give a diagnosis of the financial standing of the company.

BALANCE SHEET AS AT 31 DEC. YEAR X.

	Yr. x		Yr. x − 1		Yr. x − 2	
	£000		£000		£000	
Share Capital						
6% Preference shares	10		10		10	
Ordinary shares	50		50		50	
General Reserves	70		82		70	
Debenture	100		100		100	
Dalton Loan	52		15		15	
Deferred Taxation	63		63		77	
Profit before tax (loss)	(26)		(12)		12	
Total Liabilities		319		308		334
Fixed Assets						
Freehold property	120		120		120	
Plant and machinery	35		42		53	
Fixtures and fittings	17		23		27	
Vehicles	17		32		39	
		189		217		239
Current Assets						
Stocks	191		81		72	
Debtors	199		139		153	
Cash	–		–		–	
	390		220		225	
Less Current Liabilities						
Creditors	100		78		85	
Bank overdraft	160		51		45	
	260		129		130	
Net Current Assets		130		91		95
		319		308		334

PROFIT AND LOSS ACCOUNT, FOR YEAR ENDING 31 DEC.

	Yr. x £000		Yr. x − 1 £000		Yr. x − 2 £000	
Gross sales	560		665		726	
Less returns	10		5		5	
Net sales		550		660		721
Less cost of sales						
Opening stock	81		72		92	
Materials	331		311		299	
Direct labour	122		118		143	
Closing stock	(191)	343	(81)	420	(72)	462
Gross profit		207		240		259
Maintenance	18		17		15	
Depreciation	28		22		28	
Rates	11		10		9	
Heating and lighting	14		12		11	
Salaries	106		142		136	
Carriage	28		31		29	
Admin. expenses	8		9		12	
Financial charges	20	233	9	252	7	247
Net Profit before tax		(26)		(12)		12

CASH BUDGET, NOV. 19— to FEB. 19
(figs. to nearest £1000)

	Actual		Projected	
	NOV.	DEC.	JAN.	FEB.
Balance b/f	(135,000)	(148,000)	(160,000)	(171,000)
Income	36,000	38,000	38,000	36,000
Expenditure	49,000	50,000	49,000	49,000
Balance c/f	(148,000)	(160,000)	(171,000)	(184,000)

EXTRACT FROM NOTES TO THE ACCOUNTS

Note 7	FIXED ASSETS	Cost 000	Depreciation £000 to date	Net Book value £000
	Freehold property	120	Nil	120
	Plant and machinery	93	58	35
	Fixtures and fittings	60	43	17
	Vehicles	73	56	17
		346	157	189

EXTRACT FROM REPORT TO THE DIRECTORS

EMPLOYEES AND REMUNERATION.

The average number of employees each week is given below with equivalent figures for the previous years, together with their aggregate remuneration.

| | Yr. x | | Yr. x − 1 | | Yr. − 2 | |
	No	£000	No	£000	No	£000
Production employees	22	122	25	118	31	143
Other employees	14	106	20	142	25	136
	36	228	45	260	56	279

5. Role play: A meeting with the workers' representatives

The managers and owners of the company the famous Dalton Brothers—Alfred, Bert and Claud—have called an urgent meeting with the workers' representatives: Bill Foot, Ted Head and Tony Buckley. Everybody suspects that the former will announce drastic steps, possibly the winding up of the company. First meet in two separate groups to prepare for the confrontation.

THE DALTONS

Alfred Dalton
The oldest of the Daltons, you are very much the leader. Your special line is finance.
 In this particular instance, however, you do not quite see how you could save the situation as, pretty clearly, the plight of the company is desperate. Winding up the company seems to be the only solution. You are not too concerned as the company has been very profitable in the past and anyway you have recouped your initial investment—(£45,000 profit 4 years ago).

Bert Dalton
The youngest Dalton, you agree with your brother Alfred that the company is not worth saving unless the workers agree to massive dismissals and lay-offs—which seems unlikely. However, you would like to try to put the workers to the test so that you can pass on the blame for liquidating the company on to them.

Claud Dalton
Nicknamed "Tricky Dalton", the engineer behind most of the cleverest tricks. You agree with your two brothers that the situation of the company is pretty desperate: to carry on trading would lead to further losses. But winding up the company is going to be very costly too as the company is heavily in the red and creditors are likely to ask the parent company—the Dalton holding—to meet its liabilities. Your plan is to sell the company for a nominal sum, possibly to the workers. It would be a good publicity coup as well!

THE WORKERS

Bill Foot
You are the union's main spokesman and you are sure that the Daltons are up to their old tricks again.

You blame the management of the company for its disastrous financial position: the Moscow order was very risky; a typical case of putting all one's eggs in the one basket. You know that the Dalton holding is powerful and can back the company up until the good times return.

Ted Head
You are the union man specializing in finance. After your study of the accounts, you have discovered that:

– the company has been doing very badly for the past 3 years and is now on the verge of bankruptcy.

– however you know it has been very profitable in the past—because of low wages—It even turned out a profit of £45,000 4 years ago . . . In fact you suspect the company has been plundered by the Daltons.

– the situation would vastly improve, if you could sell the Tubchka order; this would be enough to put the company back on its feet.

Tony Buckley
You are the union man specialising in labour relations. You are used to crossing swords with the Daltons who have always taken advantage of the poor employment situation of the area to impose low wages and tough working conditions on the workers. There have been very few strikes in the past 5 years and you do not feel the workers can be held responsible for the poor state of the company. The management has committed mistakes and you don't see why the workers should pay for them. Saving the jobs is your main concern.

Part II

Evaluating the company

1. Meeting with the experts

The class will now work in two major groups:
i) experts and
ii) buyers.

There are three experts who hold specialized information on Lucky Luck Ltd. The buyers need to obtain this information in order to assess the company and propose a plan to save it.

This is an abstract of the information held by the experts.

Finance
1) sales breakdown and prices
2) stocks analysis
3) overdraft
4) age listing of debtors
5) creditors analysis
6) taxation
7) main ratios

NB *Remember to study as well the documents given in part I.*

Production
1) the production area
2) list of products
3) experience with the products
4) costs and added value
5) production process
6) machinery
7) the staff

Marketing
1) market shares
2) customers
3) customers' credit-worthiness
4) market trends
5) competition
6) advertising
7) projects

Experts
Your class leader will provide you with all the necessary documentation for your roles. Study this data carefully and use it to answer the questions put to you by the buyers.

Buyers
You have to gain as much information as you can from the experts. You will be asked to write a report on the company and decide whether it can be saved and how. Use the questions and tables which follow to help you build up a comprehensive picture of the company.

A. The products

products	sales breakdown	% of turnover	margin	market share	your conclusions

Comment on your conclusions (5 lines maximum)

B. The customers

products	who are the customers	credit-worthiness of customers	market trend	competition	your conclusions

Comment on your conclusions (5 lines maximum)

C. Production and staff

products	experience with the products	machinery	production process	the staff	your conclusions

Comment on your conclusions (5 lines maximum)

D. Finance
Study the various documents given in part 1 and with the help of the information given by the experts answer the following questions.

i) What do you think of the state of depreciation of the machinery, fixtures and vehicles? Could they be sold off at a good price?
ii) How much are the stocks really worth?
iii) Evaluate the amount of collectable debt.
iv) How much does the company own in:
   freehold property?
   plant etc.?
   stocks and work in progress?
   debtors?
v) How much does it owe in:
   debenture?
   loans?
   tax?
   creditors?
   overdraft?
vi) Has it reached its overdraft limit?

Now summarize your conclusions on the state of the company.

2. Your diagnosis
a) Can the company be saved?

```
            YES                              NO
             |                                |
           How?                            Why not?
             |
  What products would you keep?
             |
  What products would you develop?
```

b) If it can be saved how much would you be prepared to pay for it?

Part III

1. They are not fools!

The workers have decided to buy the company from the Daltons after all, but for a nominal sum: £1.

The Daltons have left all their assets as well as their liability in the company, including the loan worth £52,000.

However the company is still heavily in the red and the business press is rather sarcastic when it comments on the bold move of the workers.

From the notes given here, write an article on the purchase of the company. Use a sensational style and a critical tone.

WOULD YOU BUY LUCKY LUCK?

MASSIVE	debts to debenture holders, the taxman, its creditors, and the bank. A startling £423,000!
OLD	machinery and techniques
HUGE	uncollected debts of £199,000
USELESS	stocks made for orders which have been cancelled by Moscow
INEXPERIENCED	staff and management
A LOSS	which gets bigger every year
CASH PROBLEMS	requiring hundreds of thousands of pounds to solve.

WOULD YOU BUY LUCKY LUCK?

2. The News

Listen to this radio news bulletin.
What is the good news it gives to the new owners of Lucky Luck Ltd?

3. Pair work: A visit to the bank

To keep the company going the workers need cash. The company has already exceeded its overdraft limit by £10,000. In pairs, choose one of the roles below and act out the meeting between Pennylane and Walker. Use the accounts given in Part 1.

Mr James Pennylane, Chief Accountant, Lucky Luck
You have been commissioned to negotiate a loan from the bank.
Of course the financial situation is not too bright but the settlement with the Moscow Games committee has opened better prospects.

The company can offer little security to a prospective lender as its only real asset, the piece of land worth £120,000, is already mortgaged to secure the debenture.

However the large overdraft is going to be reduced as the cash from Moscow comes in. The new order, although it will strain the short-term cash-flow resources in the short term should also prove beneficial to the company and help put it back on its feet.

So you will ask the bank to renew its overdraft facilities up to a ceiling of £150,000.

Mr Martin Walker, Manager, Middlesex Bank

Your bank follows with some anxiety the unusual developments of the Lucky Luck affair. You are not too keen on the idea of employees playing the part of amateur managers and are not too optimistic on the outcome of this venture.

However you have to admit that the bold move by the workers has saved the company from certain bankruptcy—and this would have caused your bank to sustain heavy losses.

So you are ready to give some support to the new owners in the form of maximum overdraft facilities of £120,000. In exchange you want the bank to be represented on the board. Of course it is out of the question to consider granting any long term loan at the moment.

4. The extraordinary general meeting

The workers have become the owners of their own company. They have all become share-holders.

Study the memo opposite sent by the auditors of Lucky Luck.

Imagine you are one of the workers of Lucky Luck who will take part in the meeting.

Choose for yourself a name and a job in the company. Decide too on your age and the number of years spent in the company. Put this information on a sheet of paper in front of you.

For example:

Make up your mind on the different points listed on the agenda.

MEMO

from   Archibald Proudfoot, Chartered Accountant,
            auditor for Lucky Luck

to   Shareholders of the company   15th January 198..

1) Agenda for the Extraordinary General Meeting of January 20th 1982

   To consider :

   1. Election of 7 directors.

   2. Criteria for the distribution of shares among employees.

   3. Suggested reorganization and development plans.

2) Notes on the Agenda for employees taking part in the E.G.M.

   1. The seven directors will then elect the chairman.

   2. Three main systems can be envisaged as regards the distribution of shares among the employees

   a) pool the shares
   - advantage : the simplest solution
   - drawback : the workers will remain in a state of joint ownership. Problems will arise when employees want to abandon the pool.

   b) distribute shares evenly
   - advantage : the simplest criterion
   - drawback : the oldest employees will resent the fact that the new employees get as much as they do.

   c) distribute shares in proportion to length of service
   - advantage : fairer
   - drawback : difficult to agree on a good scale

   3. This will have to be done on the basis of the studies made last week by the consultants.

List of Business Briefs

1.	**Writing a Business Letter**	109
2.	**A Note on Memos**	111
3.	**Making a Telephone Call**	112
4.	**Booking a Flight & a Hotel Room**	114
5.	**Introducing People**	116
6.	**Welcoming Visitors**	118
7.	**Interviewing People**	120
8.	**Making Appointments**	122
9.	**Showing Somebody Round a Factory**	123
10.	**Oral Presentations**	125
11.	**Applying for a Job**	128
12.	**Understanding Financial Documents in English**	131
13.	**Negotiating/Closing a Sale**	134
14.	**How to Run a Meeting**	136–7

1. Writing a Business Letter

Layout

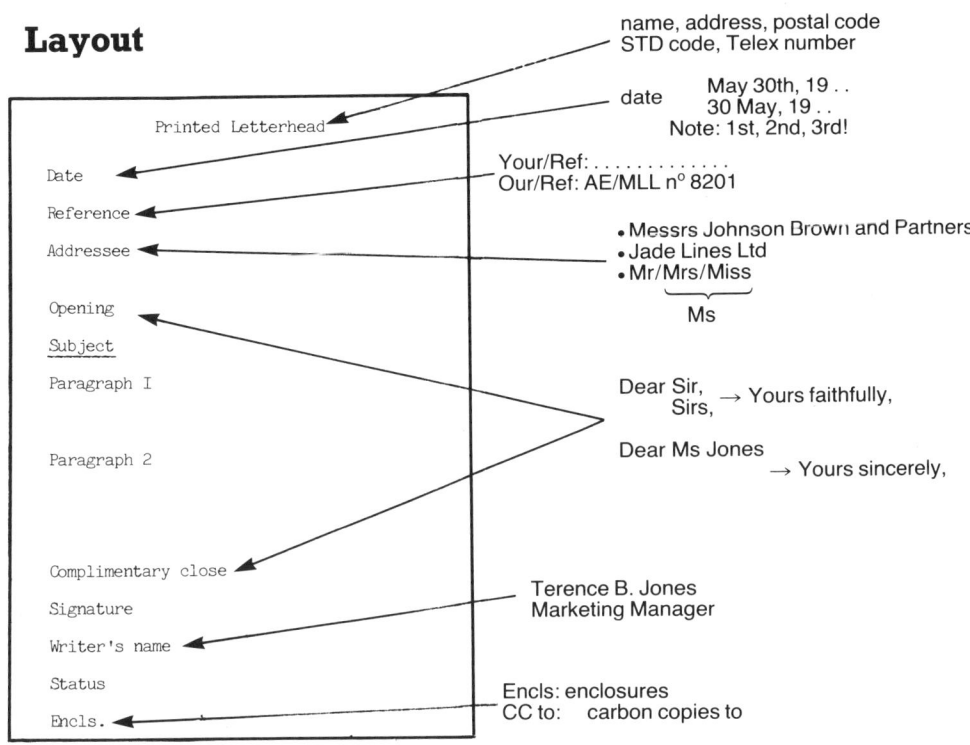

Useful phrases:

Thank you for your letter of (date)/your enquiry
Further to our telephone conversation, we enclose/please find enclosed
　　　　　　　　　　　　　　　　 please find attached/herewith
We owe your address to Messrs Pit and Jones of London and we understand
　　　　　　　　　　　　 your are currently on the market for new . . .
We look forward to meeting you on that occasion
　　　　　　　　 your prompt reply as you understand nothing can be done
　　　　　　　　　　　　　　　　　　　　　　　　　　 until then
　　　　　　　　 your visit on (date)

Avoid:

　　　　　　　　　　　　　old fashioned set phrases:

We thank you for your　　**not**　We acknowledge receipt of your esteemed favour of
letter of . . th May.　　　　　　　16th inst.

Yours faithfully　　　　　**not**　We beg to remain, Dear Sirs, your most obedient
　　　　　　　　　　　　　　　　servants.

short forms (isn't, doesn't, I'm, We're) *or over-elaborate sentences: a business letter should be short and to the point. If more details are needed we suggest a report or list of recommendations with numbered paragraphs (ex. 2.3.a:* limitations to the warranty)

Note:

Esq., means	*Mr*
Ms	*'Miz', a new accepted form that indicates only the person is female but considers that whether she's married or not is irrelevant to her professional activity.*
6th inst.	*(6th instant) 6th of this month* Note: old fashioned
cc to Jim Jones	*(carbon) copy to Jim Jones*
Encls/Enc	*enclosures (documents enclosed with the letter)*
re	*reference to . . .*

One last point:

Remember when writing to non-native speakers of English that sophisticated English may lead to misunderstandings.

Should you require any further particular . . . will probably be less easily understood than *If you need more information . . .*

2. A Note on Memos

A memo (short form for memorandum) is drafted for internal purposes and meets the need for fast internal communication within the firm. The main difference from a conversation or a phone call is that the reader will be given time to think over his reactions and will keep this document in his files for future reference. The fact that there is no coming back on what has been written and that other people may happen to read your memo should have a definite influence on the way you express things and make recommendations.

Memos are often used to inform someone of the state of things at a particular moment, and alternative courses of action may then be recommended. Memos can be addressed to a superior, a subordinate or a group of people (e.g. Memo to All Personnel in the Testing Dept). Although the style may vary according to the addressee(s), there are however basic rules one should observe when drafting a memo.

Layout

Almost all firms have got specially printed memo forms, but should you write one on plain paper, the same basic rules apply.

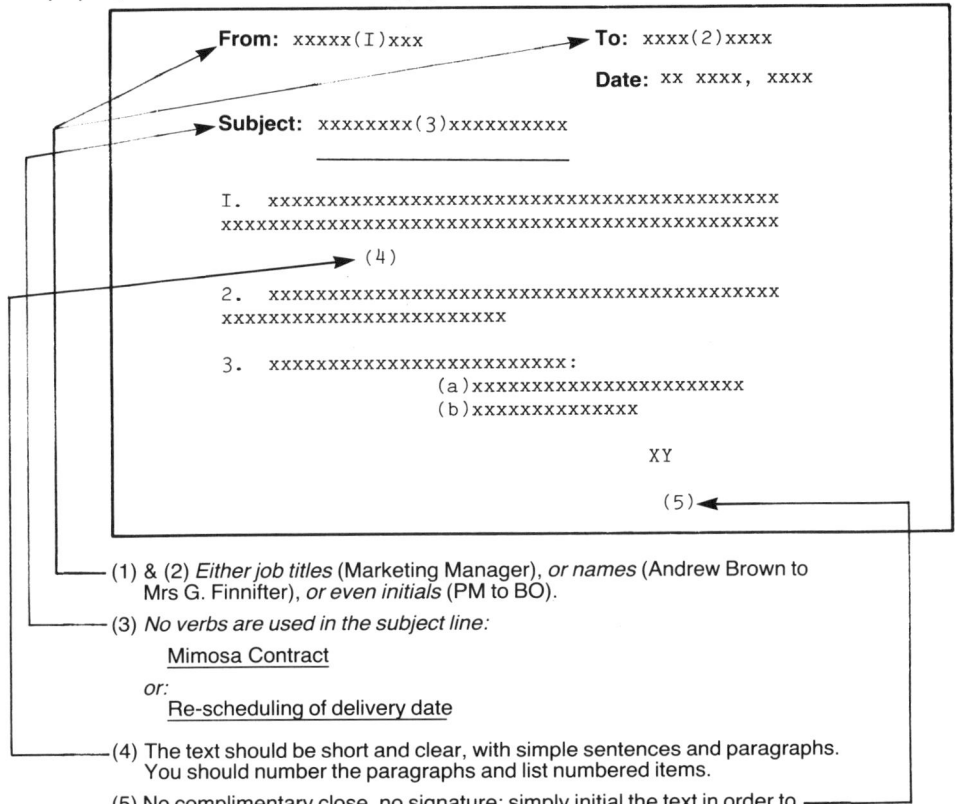

(1) & (2) *Either job titles* (Marketing Manager), *or names* (Andrew Brown to Mrs G. Finnifter), *or even initials* (PM to BO).

(3) *No verbs are used in the subject line:*

   Mimosa Contract

   or:

   Re-scheduling of delivery date

(4) The text should be short and clear, with simple sentences and paragraphs. You should number the paragraphs and list numbered items.

(5) No complimentary close, no signature: simply initial the text in order to accept responsibility for what it contains.

3. Making a Telephone Call

These expressions are used in a telephone conversation and knowing them will make communication easier.

When you pick up the telephone

Hello, Mr X speaking.
New Kitchens Ltd. Can I help you? *(from switchboard)*
Who's speaking (calling) please?
Who shall I say is calling please? *(from switchboard)*
Who would you like to speak to?
I am afraid you have a wrong number.

To get one's correspondent

Good morning. Is that New Kitchens Ltd?
Could I speak to Mr X please?
I'd like to speak to Mr X please.
Could you put me through to { Mr X please
                               { extension 304 please

To keep somebody waiting/to connect somebody

Just a { minute please
       { moment please
       { second please
Hold on } please
Hang on }
Hold the line please, I'll put you through.
I'm putting you through now.
I'm connecting you now.
You're through now.

Problems

I'm afraid Mr X is { not available this afternoon
                   { out at the moment
                   { on the other line at the moment
I'm afraid the line's engaged/busy
Could you phone (call) (ring) back later?
Would you mind calling (ringing) (phoning) back later?
Would you like Mr X to call (ring) (phone) you back later?
Would you like } to leave a message?
Do you want   }
Can I take a message?

Miscellaneous

It's urgent
There's no (great) hurry
Certainly
Of course
By all means
Fine.   O.K.   All right.   Fair enough

To finish with

I look forward to $\begin{cases} \text{seeing you} \\ \text{meeting you} \\ \text{hearing from you} \end{cases}$

Thank you for your help
Goodbye
Thank you for calling

4. Booking a Flight & a Hotel Room

Vocabulary and expressions

I Booking a flight

I'd like to book/reserve a flight from . . . to . . .
Do you have a service from . . . to . . . ?

I'd like a morning / an evening / an afternoon / an early / a late flight

When does the plane take off / leave from . . . ?

When does the plane land / touch down / arrive at . . . ?

scheduled arrival / departure time

a direct flight
the flight to Geneva calls at Paris
                    stops over at . . .

to check in luggage
check-in time

it takes an hour from the airport to the city centre (GB)
                                          downtown (US)

I like / prefer to fly British Airways/Pan Am

This flight would get you into Paris at . . .
                                      too late
                                      just in time

Flight N° . . . leaves the day before
                the same day
                the next/following day
                the day after

08.30 : oh eight thirty *or* eight thirty a.m.
11.15 : eleven fifteen (a.m. *or* in the morning)
12.00 : noon *or* twelve noon *or* midday
13.00 : thirteen hundred *or* one p.m.
14.40 : fourteen forty *or* two forty p.m.
21.10 : twenty-one ten *or* nine ten p.m.

(*Note:* Most English people still count only by the twelve-hour clock, not the twenty-four hour clock, even for official timetables. Use of the twenty-four hour clock is gradually spreading, especially for aircraft times).

Fine/Perfect/Splendid/Excellent
That will do (nicely)
That's just what I need
I'm afraid that's { no use
{ out.

II Hotel reservations

I'd like to { book / reserve } a single/double room with private { bath / shower / toilet }

I'd like to reserve for the night of . . .

a vacancy

I'm afraid I can't help you
           you'll have no choice
           we're fully booked
           we have no vacancies

Service and tax { is / is not } included
                is extra

There's a 10% service charge (on top)

a pre-paid reservation

The room will be held until you arrive
                          until 7 p.m.

Is there a night porter?

5. Introducing People

This crucial stage in social contacts is usually not given enough attention whereas it is so easy to be unwittingly off-hand in a foreign language. The language used in such occasions is rather neutral: however, it is recommended to try and bring warmth and empathy in slowing down the whole process and allowing each party to listen (and not just hear) the other's answers and react on them. The casual approach to such occasions the British adopt is a great help in this respect. Otherwise, as very often happens, the whole exercise is useless and people have to ask for much the same information again. When introducing people to one another, your role is thus to help them start their relationships in a comfortable way that will foster fruitful exchanges.

A. Introducing yourself

Good afternoon.
    morning / afternoon / evening

I'm Jeremy Hicks
My name's Hicks, James Hicks.

B. Introducing other people

neutral/formal

Ladies and Gentlemen, may I present Mr . . .
    allow me to introduce . . .
    it is my great pleasure to . . .
    honour to . . .

Mr X . . . Mr Y . . .

Mr X . . . , let me introduce Mr Y . . .
Mr X . . . , Mr Y . . . Mr Y . . . , Mr X . . .
How do you do, Mr Y.
How do you do.

Mr X . . . Mrs Y

Mr X . . . , let me introduce you to Mrs Y . . .
(ladies are considered as the more important party)

neutral/friendly

Mr X . . . , I don't think you've met Tim Hawkins, our Development Manager, have you?

Mr X . . . , this is Tim Hawkins, our Development Wizard. You'll obviously be working in close contact together. Tim, this is John X . . . our new Management Controller.
How do you do and welcome to . . . Ltd. I hope you'll like it here . . .
How do you do . . . Oh, I'm looking forward to working here after what I've seen so far . . .

C. Tips

Note: To introduce somebody *to* someone

Speak slowly when pronouncing names and give accepted short form (Robert Brown . . . Bob is our . . .)

Allow time for people to exchange a few words after their formal 'How do you do'.

Prepare a few pleasant comments in case the two are shy or slow starters.

Don't accumulate too many introductions in a very short while: this is useless as the poor newcomer is overwhelmed and will not remember anything.

6. Welcoming Visitors

A. Meeting people at the station/their hotel

Note: the effect of welcoming people personally on their arrival in the town/country is highly rewarding compared to the small effort invested.

Station
Mr X . . . , isn't it? Welcome to . . . My name's . . .
　　　　　　　　　　　　　　　　　　　　I'm . . .

Is this all your luggage? . . . Well, my car's this way . . .

How was your trip/crossing . . . I understand the sea was a bit rough . . . there was a delay in Athens . . .

Enquire whether any help is needed with what is really his concern at the moment: luggage/return bookings exchange/changing and washing/calling home. When all this has been settled, his/her mind will be much more receptive to your intended tour of the beauties of the town. When preparing the programme for the visit, don't make it too tight: allow for pauses between the various activities—prepare a small time-table with essential telephone numbers where the visitor can contact someone for help, even outside normal office hours.

Hotel (at reception)
Is Mr . . . in/Has Mr . . . arrived yet? Could you tell him Simon Jones from XYZ Ltd is expecting him in reception.
(by phone) will meet him at 6.30

B. Formal welcome

This should take place in a reception room or any such venue where tea/coffee/light refreshments can be served. It is best to allow people to wander in and invite them individually to help themselves before the formal welcome is to take place. For the speaker, it is much better to be addressing a crowd of relaxed people sipping coffee and already talking to the other members of the welcoming party than to the same timidly flocked at one end of the room and exchanging nervous comments in their own language.

　　In some cases (very formal occasions) people should wait for an invitation before making a bee line to the refreshments.

Ladies and Gentlemen, it is a great honour for us to welcome you to . . .
　　　　　　　　　　　I have great pleasure in welcoming you to . . .
(*reasons*)　First of all, because . . .
　　　　　　　A second, and I should say, foremost reason is . . .

(*wishes*)　All of us here　⎱ would like to wish you . . . and we all look forward to
　　　　　　Mr . . . and I . . . ⎰ (the results/your comments/questions . . .)

(*end joke*)　And I'm no longer going to stand between you and these refreshments
　　　　　　　　(if not yet served)

(*toast*)　　And I should like to propose a toast to . . .

(*The leader of the visiting party should answer later on with a few words of thanks on the welcome and a toast to something equivalent*)

Ladies and Gentlemen,

I have been asked (by my colleagues/my company) to say a few words
on their behalf
on behalf of my/our company.

We are $\begin{cases} \text{very} \\ \text{most} \end{cases}$ grateful to you for your $\begin{cases} \text{hospitality} \\ \text{kindness} \end{cases}$. We hope that one day we shall be able to return your invitation.
We hope that our (business) relations will go from strength to strength.

Long speeches are hard both for the speaker and the audience.
I have been told that long speeches are like wet summers: they seem to go on and on!
I do not wish to be accused of keeping you $\begin{cases} \text{from raising your glass} \\ \text{from the drinks.} \\ \text{from the bar/the restaurant.} \end{cases}$

to $\begin{cases} \text{your friends.} \\ \text{our} \end{cases}$

Let me therefore say quite simply:
　　　　We have $\begin{cases} \text{very much} \\ \text{really} \end{cases}$ enjoyed our visit. Thank you.

7. Interviewing People

Introduction (*putting the candidate at ease*)
{ Please come in
{ Do come in

Please sit down
Do have a seat
Make yourself comfortable (*friendly*)
                at home

You're Mr Jones, I believe? I'm Mr Smith.
It's Mr Jones, isn't it?

Allow me to introduce Mr X (our . . . Director) and I'm John Smith
This is Mr X (our Personnel Manager)

Referring to the CV/letter of application
I'd like to go into more detail about your CV* (if I may).
Could you tell us more about . . . ?

I see   in your CV/letter that . . . Could you tell us a little more?
You say

I gather from your CV that . . .

* What is widely known in Europe as a CV (curriculum vitae) is better known in the USA as a *resume*.

Knowledge of the firm
Could you tell us why you want to come here
                              work for us?

What do you know about our company?

How do you feel you can help our company?

What does our company offer for you?

More testing/difficult questions
What would you do if . . . ?

Let us suppose that you are the . . . Manager of our firm. What would you do if . . . ?

Let's pretend you're the Personnel Manager. I'd like you to interview me!

What makes you think you can be of use to us?

What special talents can you offer us?

What made you leave your last company?

Don't you think you are too { old   to work for us?
                               { young

What, in your opinion, are your strong and weak points?

What sort of work do you see yourself doing for us?

Don't you feel this job is more suited to a woman?
$\qquad\qquad\qquad\qquad\qquad\qquad$ a man?

What sort of salary { are you thinking of?
$\qquad\qquad\qquad\qquad$ do you have in mind?

What career do you have in mind?
What career prospects do you have?

Do you intend to make your career with us?

Do you have some questions which you'd like to ask us?

Do you like travelling?
Are you prepared to travel?

Rounding off the interview
I think we've covered just about everything. Thank you very much.

If you have no other questions, I think we'll close things here.

We'll be getting in touch with you { in the next two weeks.
$\qquad\qquad\qquad\qquad\qquad\qquad\quad$ shortly.

We'll inform you of our decision by letter } in the next ten days.
$\qquad\qquad\qquad\qquad\qquad\qquad\qquad$ phone }

We'll be contacting you . . . , { as soon as a decision has been taken.
$\qquad\qquad\qquad\qquad\qquad\quad$ once

8. Making Appointments

1. Asking for an appointment. Arranging a time

Could we meet some time soon?
I'd like to talk this over with you fairly soon; when's the best time for you?
When could we meet?
When could we get together?
When could I see you?
What time would be most convenient for you?
What time would suit you best?
Would Monday 3 o'clock { suit you? / be all right? / be convenient for you?

2. Refusal

I doubt if I'll be free then
No, Monday's { no good at all, I'm afraid / not convenient at all, I'm afraid / does not suit me at all, I'm afraid.
Sorry, I can't really make it on Monday
No, Monday's hopeless, I'm afraid
Sorry, Monday's out of the question, I'm afraid.

3. Acceptance

Yes, I could make it on Monday at three
Yes, Monday would be fine
Yes, Monday suits me very well
Yes, Monday is very convenient
Yes, I seem to be free on Monday
No, I don't have any engagements on Monday

4. Arriving for an appointment

Good morning, I have an appointment { with / to see } Mr Davies, your Personnel Manager, at 2 o'clock
Good morning, I've come to see Mr Davies, he said he would be free at . . .
I have an appointment with Mr Davies at . . .
May I see Mr Davies? He's expecting me at . . .
My secretary made an appointment for me to see Mr Davies at . . .
Good afternoon, I arranged to come and see Mr Davies at . . .

9. Showing Somebody Round a Factory

Colleagues, customers, journalists, auditors and of course competitors like to visit factories. Taking visitors on a tour of the factory or site gives you certain obligations towards your visitor: these include organising his tour, preparing him for what to expect, explaining some points, evading others, perhaps apologising, and finally saying goodbye.

Organising

This may include the invitation. It will certainly include the purpose and an outline of the route which you will follow. Useful phrases are below. Note the polite "*perhaps*", and the use of "*we*".

Perhaps you'd like to see the plant in operation/action?
It might help if we actually had a look at . . .
Perhaps we could begin by . . .
May be we could start with the _____ Dept., and then . . .
. . . and we'll be back in time for your meeting at 4.

Preparation

I'm afraid { you'll have to wear these goggles/overalls
                   this mask
              it will be rather noisy/hot/dirty

When we're in the factory, please { follow me closely
                                     don't cross the white lines
                                     don't touch any of the machines.

Just stop me if there's anything in particular you'd like to ask.

Explaining

Say what a machine or process achieves but don't go into technical details, which can bore non-experts! Use comparisons, where possible, in order to describe things.

{ In this department, we . . .
  This is where . . .

That machine works rather like a . . .
It works on the same principle as . . .

{ Without going into detail, it . . .
  Without getting technical, it . . .

Do you follow? Are you with me?

Avoiding explanations

1. Sometimes there are things you can't show, e.g. to a competitor.
". . . for security reasons"
". . . we're not authorised to . . ."
"I'm afraid it's not possible just now to visit . . ."

2. Sometimes you simply do not know the answer to a question:
I'm afraid I couldn't tell you!
Sorry, I'm not too sure about that myself!
Good question!

Apologising

Apologies in English are usually short but direct. You may not be at fault, but an apology suggests that you are at least concerned.

Sorry that { it was such a hurried visit
we weren't able to see more
you couldn't see everything in the time

Sorry about { the rush, the smell, the delay
the incident in the warehouse
your shoes

Saying goodbye

It's been a pleasure { to show you round
to give you some idea of what we do

I hope { you found it interesting
you enjoyed it
it gave you some idea of our processes

Well, goodbye.

10. Oral Presentations

Foreword

Public speaking in English is different from what it could be in the same circumstances in another cultural background. For example, understatement and informal style are rarely associated with excellence in other parts of the world, whereas they are very much appreciated by a British audience. Foreign speakers must bear this in mind to avoid appearing unnecessarily formal when making a presentation.

A talk can serve many purposes but as we are considering this in a business context, the following tips are oriented towards greater effectiveness, i.e. accurate transmission of information to a group of people.

The basics

THE 'WHAT' TEST — RESEARCH-DESKWORK
What do you wish to say? Clear your mind about the precise objectives of your speech. The result of this deskwork should be submitted to a colleague's reaction as you may have overlooked a vital point or laboured commonplace ideas.

WHO AM I? *A lucid appraisal of yourself is called for and you should define the image people usually have of you as this will influence your audience even before you open your mouth. This includes your status or role in the company. You should also review your language skills—as they will limit your range of speech techniques.*

TO WHOM? *The Audience: age, composition, past history in the company, their programme/time-table before your own appearance (e.g., will you be standing between them and their morning coffee!) and of course their likely reaction to the items reviewed above.*

WHERE/WHEN The room: size, audiovisual aids available, plugs (a good performance can be ruined by want of an adaptor), acoustics, flexibility (can the chairs be moved around), etc.
The time: you may envisage a shorter presentation if the programme is already overloaded.

HOW *i.e., getting the message across effectively to everyone in the audience. If there are foreigners in the audience, you should adapt your English to their linguistic competence. Check pronunciations and meanings.*

'D' day

IMMEDIATE HISTORY Incidents during previous speeches, striking anecdotes or themes heard so far, techniques used by other speakers. Link with what has just been done or quotation/reference to what other speakers have just said/or outside event unrelated to speech but that everybody has in mind

FEEDBACK *Reactions to your speech/theme may lead you to emphasize   insist expand OR prune/shorten/stop*

POST MORTEM Always seek short-term *and* long-term feedback, a long-term feedback being the only real gauge really—the speaker's personal charm and empathy has subsided and the vacuity of his message is then painfully obvious.

How to begin

This is a critical part of any speech as it conditions much of the attitude people will have during the whole performance.

A. Startling/paradoxical statements
This requires a keen sense of the dramatic. You should be able to use pauses, variations of speed and intonation. You should check your English carefully and rehearse as mistakes will be in the limelight.

B. Telling an anecdote
A very British way of beginning a speech.
The best start as you can adapt the story to suit your purpose but it should be short and telling in order for you to be able to draw conclusions without getting bogged down in details.

>   *Ex: As I walked out of my hotel this morning, I heard . . .*

C. Telling a joke
It should be relevant to the topic and subtle (avoid hurting the feelings of a nationality group—mock your own to be on the safe side). Remember however that jokes when translated often fall flat and that if you've heard of an English joke abroad, it is very likely so old that no one would really dare tell it again.

>   *Ex: When I was asked to speak to you tonight, I couldn't help remembering that speeches are like mini-skirts: the shorter, the better.*
>   *This reminds me, Gentlemen, of . . .*
>   *There was this French boy who . . .*

D. Referring to the immediate setting/circumstances
This is particularly important when an incident (noise outside, accident, news item, power failure) has just taken place.

>   *Ex: 'Well, if the Electricity Board will allow me to begin . . .'*
>   *'As Mr X has just suggested, I intend to . . .'*

E. The Mystery trick
Ex: I'd like you to guess where this piece of material comes from . . . Has anyone any idea about its origin? No, it's not . . .

Be careful: the thing to guess should really be mysterious and you should also be prepared for very humorous suggestions that might catch you off-balance and steal the show.

F. Involving people
You may ask people to play a small role in pairs in order to introduce your topic or perform some sort of task in groups. The danger is that they may get too involved and a lot of time is wasted or on the contrary, feel pushed and refuse to participate.

G. Stating a commonplace idea or accepted truth
This is a typical social talk gambit, but to give more power to your 'wink' you should be well aware of current affairs.

How to end

+ Give an appropriate summary or enumerate the main points.

> *To sum up . . .*
> *As a conclusion   I should like to . . .*

+ Climax the talk with an illustrative story or case study that applies what you set out to explain—this can be humorous and help end on a pleasant note.

> *As an example, I would like to tell you about what happened . . .*

If your speech has involved quoting figures and graphs, unless these are confidential, you should prepare a short hand-out summarising your points and quoting the supporting figures. Remember that figures are extremely difficult to understand in a foreign language.

11. Applying for a Job

A good general rule is to send a *handwritten* letter of application, accompanied by a *typed* curriculum vitae. The latter can be in the form of photocopies, but should be clean and clear. Nothing creates a worse effect than a dirty CV, a badly written letter and an untidy presentation. Similarly, if you decide to include a photo, make sure it does you justice. Don't use the sort which you can get from a machine at the local railway station! No photo at all is better than a bad photo. Don't forget you are trying to sell yourself, both in the CV and in the letter. It is therefore up to you to do a good marketing campaign which helps companies to see quickly the type of person you are, and how you can be of use to them. The latter is important: companies are rarely philanthropic!

Here are some guidelines on what to put in your CV, in what order, and the sort of letters you might send, depending on how you learned about the job offer (newspaper, magazine, circular letter, agency, pure speculation).

Curriculum Vitae

Name

Date of birth   Place of birth

Nationality   Marital status

Present address   Telephone number

Qualifications   Military service

Present employer

Present job *(in some detail: about a paragraph)*

Publications *(if any)*

Previous jobs *(with dates, but few details, unless the latter are important)*

Languages spoken *(say whether spoken fluently)*

Leisure activities *(not too much detail)*

Miscellaneous *(special or unusual elements you want to add)*:
    Pilot's licence, chairman of a club, membership of a professional group etc.

Referees *(names and addresses of two people who can give confidential details about your character and ability)*

NOTES.
1. Ideally you should not need more than one or a maximum of two sides of A4 paper for your CV. It must attract interest, yet leave you things to say at the interview and encourage the reader to want to meet you! Your CV may be one of dozens received, so it must stand out from the others.
2. Don't mention salary in your CV or in your letter: this must remain for the interview.

3. Your phone number is essential: most firms will try to phone you first, then confirm an appointment by letter.
4. Give your CV a lot of air, that is space out the details so that it is attractive to the eye. This is more important than most people think.
5. If you have done a period of military service, try to show this in a positive light, not as something you had to do and did not enjoy. If you had the rank of officer, say so. If you had a position of responsibility, again say so.
6. When you give details of previous jobs, concentrate on the last one. It is the one which says most about your career.
7. If you have never had a job, concentrate on any experience in industry, such as traineeships, especially if you held a post of responsibility. Similarly, the fact of having been secretary of a club is important if it means you had responsibility for taking certain decisions.
8. In English-speaking countries, it is usual to give the names, addresses and telephone numbers of people who can give information about your character and ability.

Letters

In answer to an ad. in a newspaper, magazine, a circular letter, or from an agency

Dear Sir/Sirs,
Dear Mr/Miss/Mrs/Ms

I should like to apply for the post of . . . advertised recently in The Times (12 June 19 . .)/in your letter of 12 June 19 . ./at the . . . agency.
   Please find enclosed a complete curriculum vitae.
   I should be pleased to attend an interview at any time which is convenient to you. I can be contacted at the telephone number given at any time/during working hours/during office hours/after 5 p.m.
   I look forward to hearing from you.

Yours { faithfully,
        sincerely,

D. Jones.

Speculative application.

Dear Sirs,

I am very interested in the type of work done by your company, and am at present looking for a post in this particular sector of industry. As you will see from my CV, I have some experience in this field, and would appreciate the opportunity of explaining how I feel I can be of use to your company.
   I should be pleased to attend an interview at any time which is convenient to you. I can be contacted at the telephone number given.
   I look forward to hearing from you.

Yours faithfully,

D. Jones.

NOTES.
1. In the case of sophisticated jobs, especially where you have special related experience, give further details in your letter showing why you feel you are the right person to employ.
2. Make sure your writing is clear. Large companies regularly employ graphologists to help them form an idea of candidates. Even where this is not the case, a poorly presented or dirty letter will immediately be rejected.
3. As in the CV, it is wiser not to mention salary, unless you have a very good reason for so doing.

12. Understanding Financial Documents in English

Basic accounting principles are more or less the same all over the world. In this business brief they will be summed up and peculiarities of lay-out and terminology will be emphasized.

There are three main financial documents:
1. the balance sheet
2. the profit and loss account
3. the cash flow forecast

1. The balance sheet

A balance sheet is a statement of what an enterprise owes and what it owns at a particular date. In other words it gives a snapshot of a firm's financial position.

The things a company owns are called its assets and the various sums of money that it owes are called its liabilities.

So far as form is concerned it is usual to place the assets and the liabilities on the right- and left-hand side respectively but some companies, particularly in America, reverse this order and a large number of companies set out the liabilities and the assets in columnar form.

If this lay-out is used it is current practice to deduct on the asset side the current liabilities from the current assets, so that the firms net current assets—or working capital—can be read straight from the balance sheet.

Here is a simplified balance sheet which gives only the main accounts:

LIABILITIES	£000		
Share capital			
• ordinary shares (1)	90		
• preference shares (2)	20	110	
Reserves	30	30	
Loan capital			
• debenture shares (3)	20		
• loan	30 (4)	50	
Profit (5)		10	200
ASSETS			
Fixed assets			
• land	50		
• building (6)	40		
• plant and machinery (6)	50	140	
Current assets			
• stocks (7)	80		
• debtors	40		
• cash	10	130	
Less *Current liabilities*			
• bank overdraft	40		
• creditors	30	70	
Net current assets		60	200

(1) yield a variable dividend; they are also called "equity capital"
(2) yield a fixed dividend
(3) yield a fixed interest
(4) loans are often secured by a mortgage on freehold and leasehold properties
(5) before corporation tax
(6) after depreciation
(7) or "inventories"

2. The profit and loss account

The profit and loss account is also called the working account. It records the revenue and the expenses of a company over a given financial period.

Example:

Income
- sales (1) — 900
- interest income — 50 — 950

Cost of sales
- materials — 300
- direct labour — 400 — 700

Gross Profit — 250

Expenses
- indirect labour — 120
- financial charges — 30
- selling and distribution charges — 20
- overheads: rent — 20
- heating — 15
- lighting — 15
- depreciation — 20 — 240

Net profit — 10

(1) NOTE.
Payment may not have been received for all these sales. Usually the sale is considered to be made when the goods leave the factory (or the service has been performed).

3. The cash-flow forecast

The cash-flow forecast shows how much cash the company is going to make and to need in the future.

It is an essential document when examining the solvency of a company.

Example:

Week n°	1	2	3	4
balance b/f (1)	20	30	30	20
income	60	60	50	70
expenditure	50	60	60	60
balance c/f (2)	30	30	20	30

(1) balance brought forward
(2) balance carried forward

4. Financial ratios

Comparisons between companies, or between years, may be made by means of financial ratios.

For example, the balance sheet shows us that the ratio of current assets to current liabilities is

$$130/70, \text{ or } \frac{130}{70} = 1.9$$

If next year the ratio were 0.9, the company would be less able to pay its immediate creditors.

Useful ratios include:

a. $\dfrac{\text{current assets}}{\text{current liabilities}}$ (**current ratio**)

b. $\dfrac{\text{current assets-stocks}}{\text{current liabilities}}$ (**quick ratio**)

c. $\dfrac{\text{total debt}}{\text{total equity}}$ (**leverage ratio**)

d. $\dfrac{\text{cost of goods sold for period}}{\text{average stock balance for period}}$ (**inventory turnover**)

13. Negotiating/Closing a Sale

Foreword

Many of the role playing and pairwork exercises in this book involve face to face negotiation between parties with conflicting interests. In this context, hardselling techniques and arm twisting are not really advisable, as we assume the aim of such negotiation is a fair deal that will ensure long-standing relationship.

A. DESKWORK

Do not walk into a negotiation without thorough deskwork, which means more than just reading your role cards or knowing what you are after: playing it by ear is very dangerous as you may lose sight of the overall aim of the negotiation. Above all, devote some time to putting yourself in the other party's shoes and determining what would matter to you if you were in their place. Thus you will be less caught off balance when they reveal their intentions.

B. LISTEN

Do not react too fast to proposals or suggestions. Make sure first you understand them fully—anyhow this slowing down of the process will give you time to think about your own next move. It is especially unwise to jump to a quick answer when using a foreign language as you have much more difficulty in hiding your feelings when extemporising.

Show respect for the other party and avoid crushing them when possible on mistakes/misinterpretations/etc. They would inevitably seek revenge later on at a more vital stage of the discussion. Repeat their arguments and ask for confirmation to show you understand their position before you start putting your own forward. This attitude will help you save time as very often people come back to a solution that had been suggested briefly at the beginning but had gone unnoticed.

C. COMPROMISE

At some point you must give the other party the impression they have gained something off you and praise their negotiating talents. Above all avoid strong words and emphatic language that overwhelms the other party and gets on the nerves of everyone. This can even lead to a rejection of your line of arguments as a whole.

You should however be prepared to show where you stand and refuse politely to go any further than the line of reasonable concessions.

D. CONSTRUCTIVE

Be constructive and do not stop at a deadlock—look for alternative ways of ironing out this particular difficulty. As you initiate such counter-proposals you build up an image of a constructive negotiator.

Conclusion

Remember that all of you are in business and have as much interest in a positive outcome as you are all judged on results; secondly, building up a good rapport is the best way to long-standing trade relations, which is what business is all about.

Useful language

As you are no doubt aware, this is the best . . .
I think we both realise it is in our common interest to . . .

I'll be quite frank with you: this is a deal we are indeed interested in and I feel it should be the case for you too.

I'm not sure I got everything right with regard to . . . Could you clear up that matter for me.
Maybe I didn't make myself quite clear. I was suggesting that . . .

I feel at this stage we'd better not be too specific . . .
Shall we say 10%, then?
Look, to meet you half-way, I think we could agree to . . .
In a spirit of compromise, we would be prepared to accept . . .
I'll have to refer to my head office on that point, but I'm optimistic about their answer/ I should be able to get their approval in view of the size of the order . . .

I am instructed to tell you this is very exceptional and due to . . .

I take your point but as you know we are only complying with the standard practice of our trade . . .

I have a very open mind on this matter.
As far as this is concerned, I don't think we can go along with . . .
You appreciate this is the utmost we can do to help . . .
Quite frankly, we are not at all happy with . . .

It might be a good idea to go over our terms of reference again to make sure we all agree on what has been decided.

14. How to Run

Take off

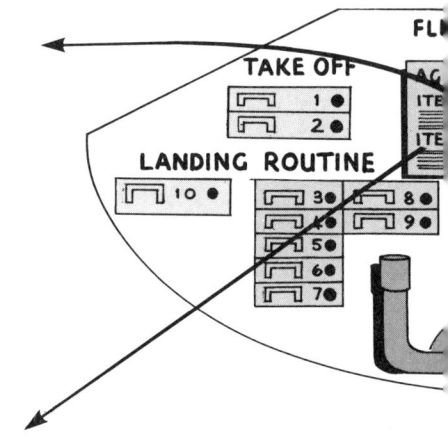

1. Opening the meeting

Informal
Right, shall we get started?
Let's make a start, shall we?
Shall we get down to business?

Formal
Good morning, Ladies & Gentlemen.
Are we all here?
I declare the meeting open.
Have you all had a copy of the agenda?

2. Setting the meeting on the right track

The issue we have to discuss today is . . .
I think we all agree that the major problem ahead of us is whether/why/where/how . . .
Perhaps we should first look at a problem/into a matter . . .
The first thing we've got to consider is . . .

The first item on the agenda today is . . .

3. Reminding people of where the matter stands

As you know/As we all know here/I understand everyone is well aware of the fact t . . .

Quite simply, the question is . . .   I would like to remind everyone that . .
Perhaps I should clarify the issue first . . .

4. Inviting somebody to express their views

Mr X . . . , as you are most directly concerned would like to come in here/on this/give us your views first/the official point of view . . .
Mr Y . . . *(rising intonation and indicating the person concerned)*
Mr X . . . , would you care to comment?

I'd like to call on Mr X . . . to present his views . . .

5. Developing a line of argument

Allow me to explain . . .
I'm sure everybody will agree that this is {an argument that carries weight . . .
                                             well worth consideration
I hope I've made myself clear on this point . . .

6. Emphasizing your point

I'd like to emphasize/stress/insist
I feel this is a vital/crucial issue
We simply cannot afford to . . .
I shouldn't like you to think I'm against this in any way, but I can't help wonderi what . . .

Landing

10. Closing the meeting

Formal
I declare the meeting closed/adjourned until 2 p.m.

I think we've covered everything . . .
Unless anyone is strongly opposed to this recommendation, I feel we should leave it there for the moment . . .
Right. You've all had your say. Has anybody anything further they wish to raise.
Can we leave the matter there then?
That's all for this morning. Thank you Ladies and Gentlemen.
I think we {might break off here.
           {might call it a day.

Meeting

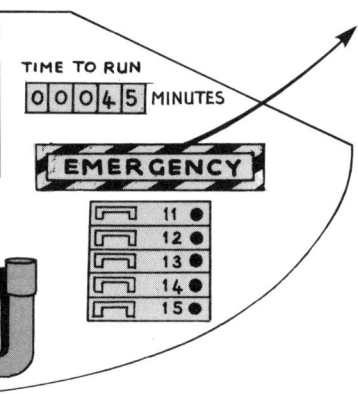

TIME TO RUN
0 0 0 4 5 MINUTES

EMERGENCY
11 ●
12 ●
13 ●
14 ●
15 ●

...viting comments

- feel free to interrupt if you wish . . .
- ...yone anything they wish to raise on this issue
  further they wish to say before we move on to the next item
- ...hat does everybody think about this? John, . . .

...mmarising

- ...em to be agreed that . . .
- ...sition as I see it is that . . .
- ...at we've all had our say, I'd like to review the position . . .
- ...point, maybe I should sum up the main points raised by all of you . . .

...ting on a motion

	Formal
...are agreed that . . . (+ should)	Are we all in favour of . . .
	That is carried then, with 6 in favour, 2 against and 1 abstention
	Mr Chairman I move that (+ subj)
	Mr Chairman I'll second that motion
	I'm afraid I won't support the motion
	With reservations.

Emergency

11. Interrupting someone

Excuse me, but I think it's relevant here to add/confirm that . . .
Forgive me, but wouldn't it be better to . . . first
I'm afraid this is not terribly relevant, Mr . . .
Perhaps we could return to your point later on . . .
We all understand your concern for . . . but our main problem now is . . . , not.
Look, I suggest we deal with this under A.O.B. . . . (any other business)
If no one objects, I should like to have a quick word on this one point.

I'm afraid we are losing sight of the main point . . .
May I draw your attention to the fact this is scheduled for this afternoon . . .
If you intend to expand on this later on, there is no need to go over it now.
I'm afraid we are losing sight of the main point . . .
          are getting sidetracked . . .

12. Keeping the discussion orderly

⎧ Hold on a moment
⎨ I'm sure you'll all   agree that we can't speak all at once. Now Mr X, could you go on
. . .
I'm sorry Mr X . . . , but Mr Y . . . was first . . .
Mr X and Mr Y . . . one meeting at a time, please . . .
Mr Z . . . would you mind addressing your remarks to the chair, please . . .
Just a moment, Mr N . . . I think Mr S . . . would like to make a point . . .
I don't think we need bring personalities into this discussion . . .
          get personal about this, do we?

Well, at this stage I feel I should summarize the matter as it stands . . .
John here thinks . . . whereas Mary would tend to prefer . . .

13. Disagreeing with someone

Excuse me, Mr X . . . , but I simply cannot agree with what you say . . .
Look, Mr X . . . , can you really expect us to believe that . . .
Hold on a minute/Just a minute Mr . . . , I'd like to come back on your last point.
I take your point Mr Z . . . and I'm sure we all do, but have you considered . . .
I was very pleased to hear that . . . but there is however one minor point . . .
I accept Mr Z's point about . . . (+ ing form), but the point is this: why . . .
I can't help feeling that . . .
To put it bluntly/To be quite frank . . . (+ something unpleasant)

14. Correcting someone

I'm afraid there seems to have been a slight misunderstanding.
Maybe I didn't make myself clear enough . . .
May I remind you that . . .
With all due respect, I've never said that . . .
Look, you know perfectly well, I've never said that . . .

15. Evading the issue

Well, that's rather difficult to say really . . .
Maybe I should finish telling yout about . . . and return to this point later . . .
No doubt this is a very valid comment, but would anybody mind if we moved on to the question of . . .
I'm afraid I'm not in a position to comment on this just yet/authorised to hand out any details on this operation . . .
Well, as a matter of fact, I was intending to deal with this later on . . .